A CESJ Paradigm Paper

The Political Animal
Economic Justice and the Sovereignty of the Human Person

By
Michael D. Greaney

© 2014 Center for Economic and Social Justice

Economic Justice Media

Published by Economic Justice Media, an imprint of CESJ
P. O. Box 40711, Washington, D.C. 20016, U.S.A.
(Tel) 703-243-5155 • (Fax) 703-243-5935
(Eml) thirdway@cesj.org • (Web) www.cesj.org

International Standard Book Number: 978-0-944997-06-2

Library of Congress Control Number: 2010907143

Cover design by Rowland L. Brohawn

Table of Contents

Introduction

For centuries the world has teetered between the chaos of individualism and the sterility of collectivism. According to whichever theory has managed to gain the upper hand in a particular milieu, the human person is considered in one of two lights. Either he is believed to be completely sovereign unto himself, with no reference to any external authority (anarchy), or, as the United States Supreme Court characterized the issue in *Pierce v. the Society of Sisters*,[1] individual identity is subsumed in the collective, and everyone becomes a "mere creature of the State." Most political and economic systems on the face of the earth today are, to one degree or another, combinations of these two extremes, variations on a theme that does an increasingly poor job of describing reality.

What is Man?

Despite the seriousness of the situation, the basic issue is not discussed to any great extent these days, nor even recognized as important. That is, What is the nature of the human person? Is humanity an anarchic species, with any social interaction directly contrary to our substantial nature? Or are we merely undifferentiated cogs in an amorphous collective, made only to serve the State?

This book started as a blog series. Originally our intent was to put down some thoughts on the nature of the human person as that term is understood within Aristotelian and Thomist philosophy. We intended to work forward from there to trace the development of the social doctrine of Pope Pius XI as analyzed by the Reverend William J. Ferree, S.M., Ph.D. Father Ferree was one of the co-founders of the Center for Economic and Social Justice

---

[1] 268 U.S. 510 1925.

("CESJ").[2] We would then rework the notes into a fore-
word for Father Ferree's landmark treatise, *The Act of
Social Justice*.[3] This is currently in editing with an eye
toward republication, as are two shorter works, Father
Ferree's *Introduction to Social Justice*[4] and *Discourses on
Social Charity*.[5]

As the reader can see from this book, the main theme
remained intact. The project, however, got a little beyond
the original scope. It went into greater detail than would
have been warranted for a foreword. The result was an
attempt to show the consistency between, even the com-
plementarity of the philosophical principles of the natural
moral law underpinning the social justice doctrine of the
Catholic Church and other major religions, and the economic justice principles of binary economics. We ended
with a description of Capital Homesteading as one possible application of the principles of the Just Third Way
that takes humanity's unique political nature into ac-
count.

Father Ferree, considered by at least one authority to
be "America's greatest social philosopher,"[6] took as the
subject of his 1941 doctoral thesis the claim that in his
writings, especially the encyclicals *Quadragesimo Anno*[7]
and *Divini Redemptoris*,[8] Pope Pius XI presented a revolutionary breakthrough in moral philosophy. This was the

---

[2] www.cesj.org.
[3] Washington, DC: The Catholic University of America Press,
1943.
[4] Rev. William Ferree, S.M., *Introduction to Social Justice*. New
York: Paulist Press, 1948.
[5] Unpublished typescript of a seminar on "Social Charity" given
by Father Ferree, Chaminade High School, Mineola, Long Is-
land, New York, April 11-13, 1966.
[6] "William Ferree: The Greatest Social Philosopher of U.S.," Rev.
Andrew F. Morlion, O.P., Ph.D., *United Peoples*, No 14, 1986, 17.
[7] Pius XI, *Quadragesimo Anno* ("On the Restructuring of the
Social Order"), 1931.
[8] Pius XI, *Divini Redemptoris* ("On Atheistic Communism"),
1937.

existence of a "new" type of virtue, social virtue, exemplified by social charity and, above all, social justice.

The difference between traditional individual virtue and social virtue is that individual virtue is directed at the good of individuals, while social virtue is directed at the common good. The common good manifests itself as that network of institutions within which humanity ordinarily acquires and develops individual virtue. This means that social virtue is specifically based on humanity's apparently unique political nature. This gave us the title of the blog series and this book, "The Political Animal," from Aristotle's[9] and Aquinas'[10] claim that man is by nature a political animal.

That being the case, the scope of what was originally intended as a piece of no more than 3,000 words rapidly expanded to bring in brief explanations of issues crucial to the correct understanding of what it means to be *political* instead of merely *individual* or *social*. Since the entire discussion on social justice is based on the breakthrough by Pope Pius XI, that also meant dealing with the specific terminology that he, as head of a global religion, used in presenting his social doctrine.

A Problem of Translation

This presented some serious problems, especially among people who hear words like "Catholic," "Christ," or "Christian," and experience a knee-jerk reaction. We could not, however, dismiss, ignore, or even bypass this terminology without compromising Father Ferree's basic thesis: that the entire thrust of Pius XI's pontificate was to present this new vision of the place of humanity in society, and the proper way to approach the structuring of our institutions in a manner consistent with the natural moral law. The pope used special terminology to explain certain concepts. If we hope to understand what the pope was talking about, we have to make the effort (welcome or not), to un-

---

[9] *The Politics*, I.ii.
[10] Ia IIae, q. 72, a. 4.

derstand what Pius XI was saying on *his* terms, not ours. Advocates of tolerance are going to have to exercise a little of the virtue that they promote. As G. K. Chesterton pointed out, it is very easy to prove someone wrong on our terms. The real test of truth comes when we prove him wrong on his own terms.[11]

Yes, such terminology may be startling to non-Catholics. It may even be obnoxious to non-Christians. As we explain in this book, even many Catholics misunderstand it. Obviously, what Catholics believe to be the pope's infallibility in matters of faith and morals does not extend to language and choice of words and terminology — or how his followers understand him. We may have to exercise our brains a little to get to the universal truths expressed in these not-so-universal terms. Hopefully, this book does that, at least in some measure.

On the other hand, you might find that you simply cannot get past the words, to the principles expressed by the words. This is a common enough problem, especially in a culture that has become saturated in legal and moral positivism. You are therefore presented with a challenge: express these principles in a manner that you find more accurate, or at least more congenial, and (assuming that what you write is consistent with the laws and characteristics of social justice, the principles of economic justice, and the framework of the Just Third Way), we will undertake to publish your work on the Just Third Way blog as a guest blogger, and, afterwards, consider republishing the material in book form.

We are, in fact, very open to surfacing new writers from all faith traditions who can accept the universal principles of the Just Third Way, with special emphasis on Jewish, Muslim, and Hindu thinkers, as well as other Christian denominations. CESJ has an interfaith membership, and would prefer that this be reflected in our publications and

---

[11] G. K. Chesterton, *Saint Thomas Aquinas: "The Dumb Ox."* New York: Image Books, 1956, 95.

other communications. We cannot do this, however, if you remain silent.

Although many statements are made about the interpretation of the natural moral law and Catholic social teaching in this book, CESJ is not a Catholic organization. Neither do the statements represent anything other than my own opinion. In no way do they represent the official position of the Catholic Church or even the Center for Economic and Social Justice, and should not be taken as such. Neither should they be considered as binding on the membership of CESJ. If nothing else, I lack the authority to make any such claim for either CESJ or the Catholic Church.

If you find yourself in disagreement with the principles or conclusions expressed in this book, we invite you to discuss them, as the CESJ "Core Values" state, "in an atmosphere of solidarity, compassion, and mutual respect." Any such discussion, adhering to the normal rules of debate and discourse, could not help but further the cause of human dignity.

1. What is a "Political Animal"?

As Aristotle declared in *The Politics*, "man is by nature a political animal."[1] We begin this analysis of man as a political animal by asking the obvious question, "What does this mean?" Aspects of Aristotle's statement do not seem to be considered today in all their depth. When we examine it, we are in essence asking what we are as human beings. We then try to understand the answer. This is a task on which we can spend our entire lives and still leave unfinished.

Individualism v. Collectivism

Because many people today tend to paint things in black and white, most responses to the question what we are as human beings usually fall into two basic categories. This is because they've decided that "political" is another word for "social," with *social* almost always construed as *collectivist*. Thus, people by and large declare the human race to be either 1) individualistic, or 2) collectivist.

Because human beings are clearly individuals, some people claim we are *only* individuals. Any organized activity is automatically "collectivism" and is contrary to human nature. They conclude that Aristotle was wrong — and not for the first time, either. Aristotle's "natural slave" argument is the quintessence of collectivism, and proves that everything he said is wrong.

Other people claim that we are only *social*. Human beings have always naturally collected themselves in groups. A number of people therefore conclude that individualistic activity is against nature; all human actions are exclusively social, the collective is everything. Aristotle managed to get the fact that we are social — collectiv-

---

[1] *Loc. cit.*

ist — right, but his over-emphasis on individual rights and virtues negates everything else he said.

As we might expect, the truth lies somewhere between these extremes. Aristotle was not wrong so much as misunderstood. He made mistakes, yes, but these mistakes were logical within his framework. They appear to have been corrected by Thomas Aquinas, for which (in part) the Catholic Church has recognized Aquinas as a "saint" (a person of exceptional holiness or "heroic virtue") and a "doctor" of the Church — someone whose learning is so great as to consider him or her an authoritative and outstanding witness to authentic Christian belief and practice.

Aristotle did not say that humanity is *either* individual or social, but is *both* individual and social. This is a combination that the Philosopher called *political*. That is, individual human beings typically gather together and associate within the structure of a *pólis*. Literally "the City State," Aristotle conceived the *pólis* as an exemplar of human social activity. The *pólis* is a system of consciously organized civic groups — institutions — within the common good. The common good finds expression as that network of institutions giving specific form to social life.

When this "social order" is adequately structured within the common good, it works to preserve both our individual nature and our social nature. Within the framework of Aristotle's thought, then, human beings are neither solely individualistic, nor exclusively social/collectivist. We are, instead, something different. Although the concept has been around for at least 2,500 years, the fact has been around forever. Nevertheless, even though we see it in action every day, many people continue to be confused by the fact that the human person appears to be something unique on Earth: a *political* animal.

Both Individual and Social

Our dual nature makes becoming more fully human confusing and contradictory if we focus exclusively either on strict individualism, or undiluted collectivism. According to Aristotle, we become more fully human (conform ourselves more closely to our own nature) when each of us acquires and develops virtue.[2] That is, when we build habits of doing good on an individual basis, but within a social context, we become more fully what we are as a combination of individual and social being. We call working out the conflicting demands between the individual and society "politics," the science of the possible.

What confuses many people is the fact that the acquisition and development of virtue is an *individual* task, but carried out within a context that requires conformity to *social* norms. For its part, society cannot force virtue on anyone. Society as a whole can, however, demand that acts affecting other individuals, groups, or the common good as a whole conform to generally-accepted concepts of virtue, regardless of the personal opinion or beliefs of an individual who thinks otherwise.

The Role of the State

The State can therefore coerce what the general consensus considers a virtuous act (though not virtue), such as paying just taxes, adhering materially to the terms of a contract, or keeping the peace. This is true whether or not the one carrying out that virtuous act is acting voluntarily and thus virtuously, or is being coerced into appropriate behavior (but without prejudice to his or her individual rights) for the common good. As important as it is for individuals personally to do good for the right motives, society is — or should be — indifferent as to whether people act in a virtuous manner (if not, strictly speaking, virtuously) out of fear of punishment, or with genuine virtue out of a desire to do the right thing and build the habit of doing good, becoming more fully human in the process. As Alexis de Tocqueville observed in his monumental *Democracy in America* (1835, 1840) when commenting on the role of organized religion in teaching and preserving the precepts of the natural moral law in the civil order,

---

[2] *The Nichomachean Ethics*, I.vii.

The sects that exist in the United States are innumerable. They all differ in respect to the worship which is due to the Creator; but they all agree in respect to the duties which are due from man to man. Each sect adores the Deity in its own peculiar manner, but all sects preach the same moral law in the name of God. If it be of the highest importance to man, as an individual, that his religion should be true, it is not so to society. Society has no future life to hope for or to fear; and provided the citizens profess a religion, the peculiar tenets of that religion are of little importance to its interests.[3]

We now need to begin looking at the implications of humanity's political nature. As we have seen, according to Aristotle, humanity is by nature neither solely individualistic nor purely social/collectivist. Humanity is, instead, an apparently unique combination of the individual and the social that Aristotle called *political*. The human condition is a paradoxical blend of *individual* rights and identity within a *social* environment. How well our institutions within the common good reflect that combination and, at the same time, are adapted to serve individual and social needs determines how effectively the social order assists each individual in acquiring and developing virtue, thereby becoming more fully human.

This sounds relatively simple. Human beings are both individual and social in nature — political. We consciously come together and organize with others in accordance with our dual (binary) nature and establish institutions to assist ourselves in the ultimate business of life: acquiring and developing virtue, that is, becoming more fully human by conforming ourselves ever closer to our own nature. That network of institutions within which we carry out the task of conforming ourselves to nature is called the common good.

---

[3] Chapter XVII, "Causes Which Tend to Maintain Democracy."

The Common Good

The common good is not an aggregate of individual goods. It is, instead, something special. The common good is so special, in fact, that it defines us as human: the capacity to acquire and develop virtue, or (as America's Founding Fathers phrased it in agreement with Aristotle[4]) the "pursuit of happiness." Paradoxically, this *general* (generic) capacity to acquire and develop virtue inherent in each human being manifests itself as *particular* institutions that provide the specific environment within which we pursue our individual good or goods. The most important of these goods is our *individual* realization of our personal capacity to acquire and develop virtue within a *social* context, thereby becoming more fully human.

This presents us with a problem. This is the same problem that faced Aristotle and which he (bound by certain preconceptions about human nature) failed to solve adequately. Not that we should blame Aristotle. People today are still making the same mistake. This mistake is rooted in the fact that it is all too common to confuse our individual capacity to acquire and develop virtue, with the institutions — social ("corporate") bodies — within which we acquire and develop virtue. This confusion seems to be the common ground on which the individualists and collectivists meet, even though they draw opposite conclusions from similar or even the same premises.

Misunderstanding Rights

The individualist understands that each of us has an individual identity and natural rights. He or she recognizes that the exercise of individual rights is the chief means by which we acquire and develop virtue. Now, keep in mind that the individualist (in common with the collectivist) confuses his or her *individual* capacity to acquire and develop virtue, with the *social* network within which we acquire and develop virtue.

---

[4] *The Nichomachean Ethics*, I.xiii.

The individualist then logically concludes that society is one of three things. These are that the State is, one, completely unnecessary but tolerable, two, a necessary evil to keep order, or three, something so contrary to human nature that it must actively be suppressed so that people can become more fully human. Institutions are, at best, only prudential. This is because institutions interfere with the exercise of individual rights. The individualistic analysis ignores the fact that rights, while individual, are just as much institutions as any other institution, and can only be realized within a social context.

The collectivist, on the other hand, realizes that institutions are necessary for each of us to acquire and develop virtue in a manner consistent with our nature. Recall, however, that the collectivist, too, confuses individual acquisition and development of virtue, with the environment within which this happens. Within his or her frame of reference, the collectivist logically concludes that individual rights only get in the way of our becoming more fully human.

To the collectivist, individual rights are thus, at best, only prudential. This is because individual rights interfere with the functioning of institutions, that is, with the mechanisms by means of which the social order operates and which give a society its specific form. The collectivist analysis, too, ignores the fact that exercise of individual rights is as fully an institution as any other institution.

The Right Approach

According to Aristotle, instead of contradicting ourselves by rejecting institutions in favor of individual rights, or dismissing individual rights to safeguard only (other) institutions, the task of the human person assembled in the *pólis* is to organize and work with others to come to some accommodation between the two competing sets of institutions. The conflicting demands of individual rights and the other institutions of the common good need to be balanced in order to arrive at an optimal arrangement between the two so that society can function. This is why politics is considered the "art" (science, really) of the possible.

There is, however, a serious problem, the solution to which ultimately eluded Aristotle — and which the failure to resolve today results in the twin errors of individualism and collectivism. That is, how can an *individual* person affect *social* institutions, and how can *individual rights* and *social institutions* both be valid and have equal claims on us?

All societies embody competing demands between individual rights and organized society. Another practical — that is, political — problem is, how can *individuals* affect *social* institutions? Isn't that trying to add apples and oranges?

The individualist believes he has the answer. That is, organized society is either unnecessary, a barely-tolerable interference with our individual rights, or a positive evil that must be eliminated for our own (individual) good. There is no question about individuals affecting the common good, because this "common good" doesn't exist. There is only individual good. *Common* good is a misnomer, an oxymoron. That is because it consists of unjustly imposing collective notions on free individuals, to their ultimate detriment. Organized society is, at best, a prudential expedient that individuals can tolerate only if they receive sufficient personal advantage from it.

The collectivist, too, believes he has the answer. That is, individual rights are an illusion, a selfish and egocentric fantasy, something that interferes with the proper functioning of the social order. There is no question about individuals affecting the common good. This is because "individual rights" do not exist. They are (at best) prudential expedients for the common good. They are granted by the State, or some agency that is the State in all but name, as deemed necessary or appropriate.

The "common ground" between these two otherwise diametrically opposed groups is their rejection of what Aristotle *really* meant, and his conception of how society and individual rights manage to integrate into a more or less common sense whole. The irony is that Aristotle's thought, while closer to reality than that of either the individualists or collectivists, embodies a serious flaw that allows the distortions of the individualists and collectivists to take root.

This is obviously a complex situation. Resolving it is not easy — although it must be possible, or basing society on the natural law as a reflection of human nature either makes no sense at all, or is an impossible task. To begin, we need to take a look at what Aristotle really meant by his statement that man is by nature a political animal.

Aristotle made his declaration that man is by nature a political animal in the first book of *The Politics*. Many authorities view the *Politics* as a continuation of *The Nichomachean Ethics*. In the *Ethics*, Aristotle examined the questions of "good" and "virtue," coming to conclusions about justice and the common good.

To summarize Aristotle's thought in the *Ethics* (too) briefly, "good" is "that for which all men strive."[5] Good is embodied the natural moral law, the basic code of human conduct. Our ideas of what is good derive from a general consensus of the entire human race in all times and places as to what constitutes "good," and consists of conforming one's self to one's own nature. "Virtue" is the habit of doing good, that is, of conforming to nature. We, of course, mean *human* nature. The Latin word *virtus* — virtue — while literally "male-ness," is best construed as "excellence in achieving human-ness." The "common good" (skipping over the long and involved reasoning) is the capacity to acquire and develop virtue, that is, humanity's inherent ability to grow and develop and thereby become more fully human.

This is fine as far as it goes. Then, in the *Politics*, Aristotle made one of his very few mistakes. This was to conclude that there are non-human beings called "natural

---

[5] *Vide* Book I of the *Nichomachean Ethics*.

slaves." These human-appearing creatures, although lacking all capacity to acquire and develop virtue, interact in society as if they *could* acquire and develop virtue. The question for Aristotle became, "How is this possible?"

2. The Common Good

In the previous chapter we saw that, due to his acceptance of slavery as a "natural" condition for some beings that are human only in appearance, Aristotle came up against a serious logical problem. That is, only persons have rights, and rights are necessary for something to be able to function in society. Rights give something a "social identity," without which no one or no thing can be a true member of or participant in society. Lacking rights means that a being has no legal — social — existence.

Things as Persons

The problem was that you had things — slaves — acting in society just as if they were actual persons. If only human beings could be persons, however, this could not be the case. Today, a "slave" is legally defined as a human being without rights, but Aristotle denied the humanity of "natural slaves"; they were "animate tools"[1] and "human only in appearance."[2]

There were thus two kinds of slaves, according to Aristotle. There were the natural slaves, who might look human but were not, and human beings who, due to some accident (meaning something other than nature), had become or been made slaves for the sake of expedience. Thus, slavery can be a permanent condition, as with chattel slavery, or temporary, as is the case when a State takes away rights from someone convicted of a crime after determination of just cause and through due process.

Aristotle concluded that somehow "things" (remember, slaves are not *persons*, but *things*), when they are owned by persons, "share" their owners' lives in some unspecified way. By being owned, a thing receives a "reflection" (we

---

[1] *The Politics, op. cit.*, I.iv.
[2] *Ibid.*, I.v.

would call it "delegation" or a grant) of its owner's virtue. This "reflected virtue" makes a thing into an extension of its owner. It enables the thing (in this case, a slave) to act in society as if it were its owner to a limited extent. "Reflected virtue" from a natural person thus makes a thing into an artificial person.[3]

Ironically, Aristotle's mistake about natural slavery was one that allowed him to make astounding advances in the science of politics that he would otherwise not have been able to make. The idea of how a government or ruler — a thing — receives a delegation of political power from its citizens — natural persons — organized into a State, is based on Aristotle's theory of how a slave participates in or shares its owner's virtue. Similarly, the whole idea of the corporation, an artificial person that is ultimately owned by natural persons, comes from Aristotle's idea of natural slavery and the problem of how a thing can be empowered to act within the social order as if it were a natural person. As we will presently see, these advances had a profound effect on Pope Pius XI's development of the doctrine of social virtue.

Acquiring and Developing Virtue

Aristotle's specific mistake was to conclude that human beings have different capacities to acquire and develop virtue.[4] The capacity to acquire and develop virtue, however, is what defines us as human — the good common to all humanity: the common good. Aristotle's conclusion that this capacity is different for every human being is extremely serious, because — if true — it means that some human beings are more human than others. Further, there are some human-appearing creatures that aren't really human, and therefore can be owned in the same way as other things.

The implications of Aristotle's error are profound. If some people are more human than others, then inequality

---

[3] *Ibid.*, I.xiii.
[4] *Ibid.*

of rights is not a problem. There are even people who have no rights at all because they have no capacity whatsoever to acquire and develop virtue. Such creatures are not, strictly speaking, human at all. They are things — natural slaves. Thus, people without the capacity to acquire and develop virtue do not participate in the common good to any degree. Those with limited or different capacities to acquire and develop virtue can only participate in society — the network of institutions by means of which the common good manifests — in a limited fashion.

As far as Aristotle was concerned, no one has or could have full access to the common good, because only a perfect being — a god — can have the full capacity to acquire and develop virtue. Paradoxically, God would have to become man in order to establish the proper relationship between the Creator and the created; humanity would have to cease being slaves of sin, that is, cease being alienated from God, and become adopted children of God in order to become fully human.

There is also a problem in Aristotle's framework with *direct* access to that complex network of institutions by means of which the common good manifests in society. To put it bluntly, it cannot be done. An exact match is necessary to fit two things together and allow direct access or interaction. You cannot force a round peg into a square hole and expect the peg or the hole to remain undamaged. Partial or non-existent individual capacities to acquire and develop virtue cannot link up with the full capacity to acquire and develop virtue — the "fullness of virtue" — that is the common good of all mankind. There is no complete or perfect "fit," and therefore no direct access.

This sets up another paradox, for the common good as it manifests in the social order as a network of institutions provides the environment within which we acquire and develop virtue . . . and these institutions are specifically manmade things. What you end up with using Aristotle's analysis is the paradox that man has created social tools — institutions — to which he has no direct access. Lacking direct access, he cannot control them or even recreate them to make them controllable, and thereby conform our institutions to their proper roles in assisting individuals in acquiring and developing virtue. If we accept the Aristotelian analysis, then, we have a contradiction: man has built a tool — the State — that is consistent with his own nature, but that is beyond his own control.

A Serious Problem

Obviously, this does not make sense. As Aristotle realized, however, man is rational. Confronted with a problem, the thing to do is not give up, but to work in a manner consistent with nature and solve the problem.

If we allow ourselves to be trapped by one of Aristotle's few errors, we are confronted with an insoluble paradox. That is, if we assume that humanity has no direct access to the common good (meaning to the complex network of institutions that make up the social order), then we have no way of improving our institutional environment. We are stuck with whatever the situation happens to be, and must make the best of it, no matter how bad things get.

On the other hand, humanity — being political by nature — creates institutions and thus a social order to assist people in the task of acquiring and developing virtue. Logically, if human beings create institutions, then human beings can reform institutions and bring them closer into conformity with our own nature. Otherwise the institutions cannot do the job for which they were intended.

The bottom line to trying to work within Aristotle's flawed framework is that we are building tools (and institutions are tools to assist us in our acquisition and development of virtue) that we can neither use the way they are intended to work, nor redesign them so that they will work as intended. We are building tools — machines (including the "machinery of the State") — that we cannot control.

Two Possible Approaches

Thus, in Aristotle's analysis people are essentially helpless before the social inertia of something that humanity itself has created. Within that framework there are only two ways to affect the common good — our institutional environment. The first is the way of individualism, or (carried to its logical extreme) anarchy. That is, break things apart and make them smaller. The current delusion of the individualist is to declare that "small is beautiful," and to demand that everything be reduced to "human scale," with "human scale" understood as *individual* human scale. This will presumably allow individuals to take charge of their own lives.

The problem with the individualistic approach (besides being completely egocentric and ultimately relativistic) is that the human person is not merely an individual, but also has a social nature, a combination Aristotle described as *political*. Anything involving even one other person is automatically beyond individual human scale. Within the "small is beautiful" paradigm, then, anything "larger" than or beyond the competence of a single, unaided human being must be eliminated if we are to follow the principle logically, that is, in a manner consistent with our rational nature. Because of our social nature, the individualistic approach is directly contrary to what we are as political animals. It leads necessarily to anarchy. Anarchy is a state of no laws, individual redefinition of laws, or each person making the decision as to which law or laws he or she chooses to obey.

The second way to affect the common good — the social order — is the way of collectivism. That is for the strongest to take charge and impose his or her will on the social order. Within the Aristotelian framework we can, however, only do this indirectly, by the strongest passing good laws and demanding obedience. This has an indirect effect on the wellbeing of all of society, the "general welfare." It does nothing directly to change or improve the institutional environment that has a specific, not a general identity. There may be (and often is) an improvement in the common good in such situations, but it cannot be directed, that is, controlled.[5]

Tentative Conclusions

In light of this observation, only two conclusions are possible: 1) the individualistic assumption that society is irredeemably evil and must be abolished at all cost for the sake of humanity, or 2) the collectivist deduction that the individual is irredeemably lost, and must be subsumed in the collective for the sake of humanity.

To recap, certain of Aristotle's assumptions about how each person has a different capacity to acquire and develop virtue lead inevitably to two conclusions about the role of the human person in society.

One, no human being can directly access (fully participate in) the institutional environment that gives specific form to a particular society. This is because there is no exact match between any individual's capacity to acquire and develop virtue, and the "fullness of virtue" that makes up the common good — the institutional environment. The institutional environment becomes accepted as a given.

Two, any individual only has indirect access to the common good, and then only if he or she has some measure of that special capacity to acquire and develop the specific type of virtue that makes a good ruler. This individual (sometimes a group, depending on the form of government) tries to make the good life (the acquisition and development of virtue) possible by passing and enforcing good laws. Our individual obedience to these laws has a generally good effect on society, while our individual disobedience has a generally bad effect.

---

[5] *Vide*, for example, the description of the "invisible hand" in Adam Smith's *The Theory of Moral Sentiments* (1759) and *The Wealth of Nations* (1776). IV.1.10, and IV.ii.9, respectively.

Legal Justice

Because the effect on the common good most often comes from obedience or disobedience to human laws, the virtue that affects the common good indirectly is called "legal justice." The idea is that when the State passes good laws and citizens obey the laws and are otherwise generally virtuous, the general welfare of society is improved. Because legal justice does not act directly on its object — the common good — it is not a *particular* virtue, but a *general* virtue.

The terms "particular" and "general" have a special meaning in this context. A particular virtue is one that has an identifiable "act" necessarily directed at a "person" as its object. This means that the practice of the virtue requires that it affect a *person* directly.

A general virtue, on the other hand, only affects its object indirectly, and has no identifiable "act." The *quasi*-act of a general virtue (if it may be so described) is the "fall-out" that the practice of particular virtues has on the common good, at least that part of it referred to by the American Founding Fathers in the United States Constitution as "the general welfare."

Now, because this legal justice does not act on or "look" directly to its object, there is no specific ("particular") act that can be identified as an "act of legal justice." Instead, the "act" of legal justice can at best be described as the indirect effect that the acts of other virtues have on the general welfare of society.[6]

---

[6] *Vide* Ferree, *The Act of Social Justice, op. cit.*, 9-31, esp. "St. Thomas' Analysis of Legal Justice," "For Aristotle, . . . legal justice was simply another name for virtue taken as a whole, a name which applied to the whole of virtue insofar as it was 'towards another,' and for this reason an act of some other virtue would *always* have to be present before legal justice could be present, for legal justice would be *that act of some other virtue* in its relation to one's neighbor. It may, indeed, be seriously questioned whether it is proper at all to speak of an 'act' of legal jus-

It becomes evident, then, that this thing we call the common good has two aspects, one "particular," that is, specific, concrete, and identifiable, and the other non-specific and "general." The particular aspect of the common good is the network of institutions — including laws, customs, traditions, and so on — that give specific form to the social order within which we as political creatures work to become more fully what we are.

The general aspect of the common good — the "general welfare" — on the other hand, can possibly best be understood as the "tone" of a society: not just that good laws are being obeyed, but *how* they are obeyed, and even the quality of the laws themselves. Are the laws that are being passed, in fact, good laws? Even if they are clearly good laws, are people obeying them in the manner in which the lawmakers intended they should be obeyed, and are the laws having the desired effect?[7]

When Things Can Be Persons

In the Aristotelian framework, we thus have a paradox. We cannot act specifically (directly) on the common good whether or not it has a specific — "particular" — identity. In philosophy and law, only a "person" can be the directed object of an "act." This is because only persons have rights. If we (in colloquial terms) perform an act that injures or benefits a thing — a non-person or that which has no rights — the goodness or badness of that act in legal or social terms is not the goodness or badness of the effect that our act has on the thing. Rather, the goodness or badness of our act (again, in legal or social terms) is determined by how our act affects the person whose rights to and over that thing have been injured or benefited.

Aristotle "solved" this problem by observing the institution of slavery. Seeing that slaves — "animate tools" —

---

tice in Aristotle's sense, any more than it would be proper to speak of an 'act' of metaphorical justice." (29)

[7] *Vide* Albert Venn Dicey, *Lectures on the Relation Between Law and Public Opinion in England in the Nineteenth Century*. New Brunswick, Connecticut: Transaction Books, 1981.

functioned in society on behalf of their owners as if they *were* their owners, Aristotle claimed that, in cases in which a thing functions in society as if it were a person, the thing becomes, in effect, an artificial person by reason of the reflection of virtue from its owner, and the exercise of rights on behalf of its owner.

A thing, of course, cannot be a *natural* person in its own right. A thing, however, can be an *artificial* person by a delegation of rights from its owner or (in the case of a political entity) its sovereign. This, obviously, says nothing about whether slavery is right or just. It is simply the theory that Aristotle developed to explain how, given the fact of slavery, a slave — or anything else that is not a natural person — manages to participate in the common good, even though a slave is not a person, but a thing.

In political matters (using the word in its modern sense) the identity of a sovereign in a State may be an issue, *e.g.*, whether the people or a divine right ruler. The bottom line in any political arrangement, however, is that the State — a thing — must derive its just powers from a natural person or persons somewhere along the line.

Similarly, there can be multitudes of artificial persons in society, such as slaves, charitable foundations, or business corporations, but somewhere there has to be a natural person or persons from which these artificial persons derive the rights that they exercise. In addition, it is a basic principle of law that no one (or thing) can acquire greater rights than the person granting those rights has in the first place. If, for example, you owe me a debt of five dollars, I cannot assign or grant the right to collect five dollars to my neighbor as a debt of ten dollars that my neighbor then collects from you.

The Corporation

The act of creating an artificial person has a special word in philosophy: incorporation. This is probably a bad word, for today it is used almost exclusively to refer to business corporations and, on rare occasions, to political entities at the municipal level. We are going to have to use it, however, for the word was used in the 17th century in the development of totalitarian political philosophies to describe any organization that interposed between the State and the individual. It is thus critical in the development of theories that countered those philosophies.

That, however, is a subject for later discussion. In our next chapter we will begin looking at how Aquinas corrected Aristotle's error — though not the effects of the error or its continued widespread acceptance throughout the world.

3. The Individual and Society

As we have seen, what was possibly Aristotle's most serious and fundamental error is his conclusion that each individual human being has a different capacity to acquire and develop virtue. Logically, then, while in Aristotle's framework no one is fully human in the sense that he or she possesses the full capacity to acquire and develop virtue, some people have a greater capacity to acquire and develop virtue than others. Such individuals are thus more human than others. Still others, while human in appearance, completely lack any capacity to acquire and develop virtue. They therefore also lack the natural rights the exercise of which is essential to the acquisition and development of virtue. These are the natural slaves.

All Humans are Fully Human

With the coming of Christianity, however, a new understanding of what it means to be human came on the scene, although (in justice) Christianity cannot be said to have originated the idea. Christianity views itself as the fulfillment of Judaism, so it should come as no surprise that what we see in Christianity can be found also in Judaism. These ideas did not spring full-grown with the birth of Christianity. Credit rightfully goes to the Jews.

Judaism, however, was (by and large) viewed as being exclusively for Jews. Whatever the purely religious claims of Judaism and Christianity and the differences between them, the basic understanding of what it means to be human is essentially the same in both religions, as well as in Islam. In a natural (that is, non-religious) sense, Christianity's contribution was to universalize Judaism's view of the human person and his or her role in society. The Law — meaning the natural moral law — was no longer to be understood or construed as something exclusively for Jews, but, when reduced to its essential precepts, as applying to the whole of mankind. As Jesus tried to make clear, He came to fulfill the Law, not to abolish it; not the tiniest particle of the Law would pass away.[1]

Aside from the revolutionary idea that there is only one God, then, Judaism seems to have popularized the idea (also found in some of the Sophist philosophers, although, if we believe Aristotle, evidently poorly argued) that every human being is as fully human as every other human being. That is, each human being has the same capacity to acquire and develop virtue as every other human being. All human beings are thus fully human, and all human beings therefore meet the requirements for full participation in the common good.

The Rediscovery of Aristotle

This new view of humanity caused a serious problem when the philosophy of Aristotle was "rediscovered" in the 12th century. The philosophy of Aristotle was clearly based on logic and common sense, and yet appeared to be in conflict with the truths of revealed religion. In a line of argument that has been labeled "buffoonery," at least one commentator, Siger of Brabant, tried to explain away this problem by asserting that there are thus two different truths, one religious, and one scientific. In this Siger was ably opposed by Aquinas — although who is to be the ultimate victor appears to be in doubt to this day. As G. K. Chesterton described the matter,

> Siger of Brabant said this: the Church must be right theologically, but she can be wrong scientifically. There are two truths; the truth of the supernatural world, and the truth of the natural world, which contradicts the supernatural world. While we are being naturalists, we can suppose that Christianity is all nonsense; but then, when we remember that we are Christians, we must admit that Christianity is true even if it is nonsense. In other words, Siger of Brabant split the human head in two, like the blow in an old

---

[1] Matthew, 5:18.

legend of battle, and declared that a man has two minds, with one of which he must entirely believe and with the other may utterly disbelieve.[2]

Among other issues (which, however important, we will not get into here), Aristotle's conclusion that each human being has a different capacity to acquire and develop virtue and some have none, came into direct conflict with the Christian idea that all human beings have the same ("analogously complete") capacity to acquire and develop virtue — the equal opportunity and means to become "adopted children" of God. As America's Founding Fathers were to put it later, "All men are created equal."

The Analogy of Being

In response to the oddities propounded by Siger of Brabant and to resolve the apparent paradox presented by Aristotelian philosophy, Aquinas posed his theory of "analogy of being." That is, each and every human being is "analogously complete" with respect to every other human being. If you are human, you are fully human. If you are not human, you are fully not human. Whatever anything is, it is fully whatever it is, without qualification. If a thing is a particular thing, it is fully that thing. If it is not that thing, it is completely not that thing.[3]

Aquinas's analogy of being is a logical development of Aristotle's "principle (or law) of contradiction" (or noncontradiction): nothing can both "be" and "not be" at the same time. Thus, Aristotle's theory that human beings can have different capacities to acquire and develop virtue — the capacity to acquire and develop virtue being that which defines us as "human" — does not hold water in light of his own law of contradiction.

Reconciling the Individual with Society

This breakthrough of Aquinas laid the groundwork for reconciling the individualistic and the collectivist views of

---

[2] G. K. Chesterton, *Saint Thomas Aquinas: "The Dumb Ox."* New York: Image Books, 1956, 92-93.
[3] I q. 1 a. 3.

society. He resolved this conflict in an unusual way, an extremely subtle technique by means of which he did not disagree with Aristotle directly. Instead, Aquinas carefully avoided undermining Aristotle's authority by explaining what Aristotle *really* meant by a passage that appeared to be in conflict with essential Christian precepts.[4]

For example, Aristotle was rather clear what he meant when he said that some human-appearing creatures lack all capacity to acquire and develop virtue, and are thus "natural slaves." In the *Summa*, however, Aquinas explained that what Aristotle *really* meant is that there are some people, such as criminals, who (due to some accident in their makeup or their upbringing) are not adequately realizing their analogously complete capacity to acquire and develop virtue. They are dangers to themselves and to society, and are therefore in need of training and correction so that they can be fitted to reenter civil society.[5]

Thus (so Aquinas claimed) what Aristotle *really* meant when he said that some men are "natural slaves" is something different from what we might suppose. Aquinas explained that what Aristotle meant is that, when someone is clearly in need of correction and rehabilitation in order to be able to function adequately in society, it is natural that such an individual be deprived of the exercise of rights and put in the care of a master — the State or a private individual. The master is responsible for undertaking the task of rehabilitating the criminal and training him or her to reenter society. In this way Aquinas managed to maintain the Judeo-Christian belief in humanity's analogously complete capacity to acquire and develop virtue, but without appearing to contradict Aristotle's natural slave argument.

Aquinas did something similar with legal justice. In the treatise on law in the *Summa*, the "Angelic Doctor" laid out Aristotle's argument on legal justice. Aquinas carefully explained how legal justice is a general, not a particu-

---

[4] Ferree, *The Act of Social Justice, op. cit.*, 21.
[5] IIa IIae, q. 57, a. 3.

lar virtue. Thus, while legal justice has the common good as its object, the common good is not the *directed* object of legal justice. That would be impossible, for legal justice is a *general* justice, and therefore cannot have a *particular*, that is, a *directed* act. Instead, the *quasi*-act of legal justice consists of the indirect beneficial effect that the acquisition and development of *other* virtues has on the common good.

The Helplessness of the Individual

So far, so good. Aquinas was evidently in full agreement with Aristotle. As we have seen, however, implicit in Aristotle's analysis (and thus in Aquinas's apparent agreement with Aristotle) is the presumption that, if the virtue that has the common good as its object — legal justice — is and can only be indirect, then two conclusions are inevitable. One, human beings do not have analogously complete capacities to acquire and develop virtue, and therefore do not have equal rights. Two, no one has direct access to the common good, that complex network of institutions within which we acquire and develop virtue, and the social order is therefore a given and unchangeable through human effort. Individuals are helpless to effect changes directly for good or for ill in the social order.

The individualist resolves this conflict by rejecting the social order as a positive good in conformity with nature. At best, the individualist tolerates the State as a necessary evil, as prudential matter, but only up to the point where infringement of individual rights becomes intolerable.

The collectivist takes the opposite approach. He or she resolves the conflict by rejecting individual rights as positive goods in conformity with nature. At best, the collectivist tolerates individual rights as necessary evils, as prudential matter, up to the point where the exercise of individual rights becomes intolerable.

A Different View

Aquinas presented us with a different solution, as William Ferree, S.M., Ph.D., pointed out in *The Act of Social*

Justice.[6] What Aquinas did was extremely subtle, and appears to have been missed for eight centuries. Of course, we also have to consider the possibility that Aquinas's solution might be in a section of the *Summa* that Aquinas did not complete. It may be one of the passages "filled in" by his students from his notes and other writings.[7] It might therefore be not so much subtle as too brief, coming across as a simple unimportant assertion without explanation.

Whatever the reason, after presenting Aristotle's classic analysis of legal justice in the *Summa* (keep in mind that Aristotle's main point is that legal justice is a general virtue and can only affect the common good indirectly) Aquinas makes the single — and astounding — statement, "Legal justice alone looks *directly* to the common good."[8] The implications of this brief statement are profound and yet have been largely ignored since Aquinas made it.

It is not just that Aquinas seemed to have contradicted everything he had just said with respect to legal justice. If legal justice looks *directly* to the common good, then much of what Aristotle concluded about how people participate in the common good is wrong. Instead of having no power to affect the institutions of the social order, or being forced to relegate all power over the common good to the State or an economic or political elite, the common good is, on the contrary, directly accessible by every single human being.

Who, then, is correct? Aristotle, who claimed that some people are only partially human (and some not human at all), and that in consequence the common good is not directly accessible by anyone? Or is Aquinas correct — Aquinas, who contradicted Aristotle's idea that some people could be less than human, but then agreed with Aris-

---

[6] Ferree, *The Act of Social Justice, op. cit.*, "St. Thomas' Analysis of Legal Justice," 9-31.

[7] Teodoro de la Torre, *Popular History of Philosophy.* Houston, Texas: Lumen Christi Press, 1988, 112.

[8] Ia IIae q. 61 5, 4m.

totle about legal justice and the inability of anyone to have direct access to the common good . . . and then seems to have turned around and contradicted himself?

4. The Role of the State

In the previous chapter we saw that Aristotle and Aquinas both agreed and disagreed on their respective understandings of legal justice and how people participate in the common good. According to Aristotle, no one has direct access to the common good by means of an act of a virtue. According to Aquinas, no individual *as an individual* has direct access to the common good by means of an act of a virtue . . . but that the common good is directly accessible. How is this possible?

Understanding Terminology

Unfortunately, Aquinas did not explain how the common good is both not directly accessible by any act, and is directly accessible . . . but not by any *individual* act. (Remember this, for it is an important point: no individual *as an individual* can have direct access to the common good.) To this we need to add the general principle of philosophy that no one other than a person can carry out an act of a virtue. Further, no one can act directly on something that does not allow a particular act — and a general virtue is, by definition, a virtue that does not have a particular act.

The solution to the first of Aquinas's apparent self-contradictions becomes evident once we think about it. If you have something you call legal justice that you define as a *general* virtue with the common good as its indirect object, and then claim that legal justice alone looks directly to the common good and is thus a *particular* virtue, it is clear that you are using the same term for two different things. Obviously, then, Aquinas was telling us that there is a *general* virtue called legal justice that has the common good as its indirect object . . . and that there is a *particular* virtue, that he also confusingly called legal justice that has the common good as its *direct* object. Logically,

there are thus (according to Aquinas) *two* distinct types of
legal justice, one general, and one particular.

Two Types of Legal Justice

General legal justice is just what Aristotle said it is: a
general virtue without a directed (particular) act that has
the common good as its indirect object. Particular legal
justice, however, has the common good as its directed object — "legal justice alone looks *directly* to the common
good" . . . and there Aquinas leaves us hanging. It necessarily follows from the fact that a virtue is a particular
virtue that it has a directed act . . . but all we can tell
from what Aquinas said following his declaration about
particular legal justice is, although particular legal justice
has a directed object, individuals as individuals cannot
carry out a directed act of legal justice! (Again, this is a
critical point to keep in mind: individuals *as individuals*
cannot carry out directed acts of legal justice.)

The "act" of legal justice, whether general or particular,
apparently remains the non-specific, indirect effect that
Aristotle described. That is, the effect that individuals
acquiring and developing the classic virtues has on the
general welfare. The "act" of legal justice is not any particular, directed effect on the complex network of institutions that make up the concrete manifestation of the
common good and give specific form to the social order.

For the next eight centuries or so philosophers and political scientists got around this difficulty by . . . ignoring
it. Treatises on justice examined legal justice exclusively
as a general virtue (and not very deeply, as Ferree
ed[1]), and left it at that. The only way to affect the common
good, they concluded, is indirectly, and then only by
means of acts of other virtues that somehow improve the
general welfare of the community.[2] In the meantime,
however, a theory was reemerging in Europe regarding

---

[1] Ferree, *The Act of Social Justice, op. cit.*, 80-83.
[2] *Ibid.*, 37-76.

the origin and transmission of political power — sovereignty.

Three Human Societies

For centuries the west had more or less based its politics on Roman theory. According to the Romans, the social order is divided into three discrete societies, domestic (the family), religious (the temple), and civil (the State). Sovereignty is a slightly different concept, or at least has different applications, in each of the three societies.

In the family, the Romans believed the gods vested all power over domestic matters in the head of the family, the *pater familias*. No one, not even the head of State or the chief priest, could interfere with the power of life and death that the *pater familias* exercised over the members of his *familia*. In theory, anyway. In practice, it wasn't too uncommon for a *pater familias* to be prosecuted for violating a family member's civil or even religious rights, such as poisoning your wife or introducing the worship of unauthorized gods into the family. Even a slave had the *quasi*-right to sue for his freedom if he thought he could prove he had been unjustly enslaved — and winning such a case was not as rare as we might think.[3]

Religious society was similar. The gods vested the priest with the power to administer religious matters. With so many gods, however, and the fact that the Romans were always bringing in new ones as new nations joined or were brought into the Empire, it was anybody's free choice which god or gods you worshipped, or even whether you worshipped at all. Again, that was the theory. In practice, many civil institutions, such as the games, had a *quasi*-religious character, and required participation by religious authorities or religious sanction.

Foreign affairs, for example, were construed as relations between peoples under the protection of different

---

[3] *Vide* the extended discussions in J. A. Crook, *Law and Life of Rome, 90 B.C. - A.D. 212*. Ithaca, New York: Cornell University Press, 1967.

gods, so diplomats at the highest level had to be priests. Also, the person of a diplomat or envoy was considered sacred, so harming a diplomat offended the god or gods involved. A witness could not give testimony in a court of law without calling a god — usually Apollo — to stand surety, and to punish the witness in the next life if the testimony was perjured. When the reigning Cæsar was considered divine or at least semi-divine, soldiers burned incense to the emperor's "genius," symbolized by his bust, as a test of loyalty. Early Christians were considered dangerous atheists and traitors to the State for refusing to participate in these practices.

In civil society, however, the Romans believed all power resides in the people. The State receives its power as a grant from the people who make up the State. The Romans don't appear to have gone much further than that, but the principle is clear. A particular State only exists by the consent of the governed, and the selection of ruler is ultimately the people's choice — in theory. "Emperor" (*Imperator*) was not a civil office, but a military honor signifying "one worthy to command Romans in battle." The Heads of State (there were always two) were officially the Consuls, in theory elected every year. How well this worked in practice, and how consistently it was applied is a different issue.

No Divine Right to Rule

The bottom line in all this is that during the Middle Ages, any ruler, regardless of the specific form of government, was believed to rule ultimately only with the consent of those whom he or she ruled, albeit with the sanction of God, sometimes confusingly referred to as ruling by "divine right."[4] With the intellectual revolution that

---

[4] *Vide, e.g.,* "Two sons survived him [Pepin], Charlemagne and Carloman, and on these the succession of the kingship devolved by divine right. A general assembly was convened, according to custom, and the Franks appointed the two of them to be their Kings." The second sentence contradicts the first sentence if we understand "divine right" in the modern or post-Reformation

resulted from the rediscovery of Aristotle in the 12th century and in response to the changing political situation, however, new theories began to evolve or old ones to be revived as philosophers and political scientists began to examine the matter in greater detail.

Thus, in 1896 (the same year in which he entered the Community of the Resurrection at Mirfield), the Anglican monk John Neville Figgis (1868-1919) published *The Divine Right of Kings*, a study of the political philosophy that reached the height of its development after — and as a result of — the Reformation.

From the Catholic point of view, the Mirfield Community (which still exists) is a relic of the somewhat artificial effort initiated during the "Oxford Movement" to revive the role that the monasteries had in the daily life of the people prior to what is euphemistically described as "the break with Rome." It is an application of "branch theory," a complicated issue that has no real significance for our argument, however important it might otherwise be. Whatever might be your personal opinion of such efforts as the Community of the Resurrection, it attracted some of the leading intellectual lights of the Anglican Church. The popular novelist Robert Hugh Benson (1871-1914) spent time there before his conversion to Catholicism and ordination as a Catholic priest.

Figgis's scholarly labors took a different direction. While apparently convinced to the end of his days of the falsity, *etc.*, of the claims of "the Church of Rome" to a spiritual supremacy in Christendom, in all honesty he openly admitted, in common with William Cobbett a century earlier, that essential concepts such as the natural equality of all men, democracy, and governing with the consent of the governed had all been developments and teachings of the "Church of Rome" to which (for expedience, if nothing else) we will refer in the customary fashion as "the Catholic Church." (Some authorities consider

---

sense. Einhard and Notker the Stammerer, *Two Lives of Charlemagne*. London: Penguin Books, 1969, 57.

the term "Roman" Catholic to be a concession to "branch theory," that is, to the belief that there are three "branches" of the Universal — Catholic — Church: Orthodox, Roman, and Anglican. The autocephalous Orthodox churches and the churches in union with the pope do not accept branch theory.)

Figgis concluded that divine right theory is a purely Protestant invention, and directly contrary to the great philosophical and political tradition of the West. While he utterly rejected the claims of the Catholic Church relating to the supremacy of the pope, Figgis felt himself compelled to admit (in agreement with Algernon Sidney) that, as far as political theory went, the Catholic Church was in the right. The Catholic Church was, and had always been, a champion of political democracy as the theory most consistent with the dignity of the human person.

Paradoxically, however, many people today, even (or especially) devout Catholics, seem unalterably convinced that a divine right monarchy is the only legitimate "Catholic" form of government, the only form given direct sanction by God Himself, and the only form approved by the Vatican and the papacy. How this came to be is the result of a series of historical accidents, as well as the triumph (temporary, we hope) of the party that since the sixteenth century has sought to base the natural moral law on God's revealed Will (explicit commands of God found in documents we accept on faith), rather than on His Intellect (divine Nature reflected in that of every human being and discerned by reason alone). It is a complicated story, but we will try to condense it as best we can.

The Triumph of the Will

It begins, as we might expect, with the rediscovery of Aristotelian philosophy in the 12th century — something to which we will keep returning in order to understand what is going on in the modern world. As Dr. Heinrich Rommen explained in his book, *The Natural Law,*

> With Duns Scotus (d. *cir.* 1308), and with the principle of the primacy of the will over the intellect so

much emphasized by him, there began inside moral philosophy a train of thought which in later centuries would recur in secularized form in the domain of legal philosophy. The principle that law is will would be referred in legal positivism, as well as in the theory of will in jurisprudence, to the earthly lawmaker (self-obligation).

For Duns Scotus morality depends on the will of God. A thing is good not because it corresponds to the nature of God or, analogically, to the nature of man, but because God so wills. Hence the *lex naturalis* could be other than it is even materially or as to content, because it has no intrinsic connection with God's essence, which is self-conscious in His intellect. For Scotus, therefore, the laws of the second table of the Decalogue were no longer unalterable. The crux of theology, namely, the problem of the apparent dispensations from the natural law mentioned in the Old Testament and thus seemingly granted by God (the command to sacrifice Isaac, Raphael's apparent lie, Osee's alleged adultery, the polygamy of the patriarchs, and so on), was now readily solved. Yet St. Thomas, too, had been able to solve such cases. Now, however, an evolution set in which, in the doctrine of William of Occam (d. *cir.* 1349) on the natural moral law, would lead to pure moral positivism, indeed to nihilism.[5]

Rommen was a student of the great Father Heinrich Pesch, S.J., Ph.D., who (in common with so many thinkers of equal or even greater caliber) has suffered much at the hands of later commentators and disciples who twist the otherwise clear teachings of their "master" to fit their own preconceived theories and ideas. The distortions forced on the distributism of G. K. Chesterton and Hilaire Belloc come forcibly to mind, especially those that change the substantial nature of natural rights to liberty — freedom

---

[5] Heinrich Rommen, *The Natural Law*. Indianapolis, Indiana: Liberty Fund, Inc., 1998, 51-52.

of association — private property, and pursuit of happiness — the acquisition and development of virtue.

As a member and co-organizer of the renowned *Königswinterkreis* discussion group that included such luminaries as Father Oswald von Nell Breuning, Gustav Gundlach, and Franz Müller, Rommen was probably more "in touch" with Father Pesch's teachings than some authorities today who seek to validate their personal opinions at the expense of common sense and sound philosophy by using Father Pesch's name as a deodorant for systems that are socialism in all but name.

The Overthrow of Reason

The Occamist "triumph of the Will" that developed out of distortions of the thought of Duns Scotus and which led to the development of socialism received its greatest impetus as a result of the success of the Reformation. This was due in large measure to the fact that by the 17th century the Protestant groups finally saw themselves as completely separate bodies from Rome, and ceased looking to Rome for philosophical as well as theological guidance.[6] The thought of Aristotle and Aquinas was replaced with new philosophies. As that genial commentator of the early 20th century, G. K. Chesterton, commented,

> Since the modern world began in the sixteenth century, nobody's system of philosophy has really corresponded to everybody's sense of reality; to what, if left to themselves, common men would call common sense. Each started with a paradox: a peculiar point of view demanding the sacrifice of what they would call a sane point of view. That is the one thing common to Hobbes and Hegel, to Kant and Bergson, to Berkeley and William James. A man had to believe something that no normal man would believe, if it were suddenly propounded to his simplicity; as that law is above

---

[6] *Vide* the analysis by Hilaire Belloc, *How the Reformation Happened*. Magnolia, Massachusetts: Peter Smith Publishers, Inc., 1975.

right, or right is outside reason, or things are only as
we think them, or everything is relative to a reality
that is not there. The modern philosopher claims, like
a sort of confidence man, that if once we will grant
him this, the rest will be easy; he will straighten out
the world, if once he is allowed to give this one twist
to the mind.[7]

---

[7] G. K. Chesterton, *Saint Thomas Aquinas, "The Dumb Ox."*
New York: Image Books, 1956, 145-146.

5. The Basis of Natural Law

In the previous chapter, we found that many people base their understanding of the role of the State and the place of man within the common good on a theory of human society peculiar to themselves. Almost inevitably these theories are irreconcilable with the traditional Aristotelian and Thomist understanding of the natural moral law based not on the Will, but on the Intellect, that is, on reason alone.

The Problem with Will

Within the framework that bases the natural law on the Will, "right" and "wrong," as Heinrich Rommen pointed out, become matters of opinion. Morality becomes "situational," based on the personal faith of the individual with little or no reference to reason or common sense. Reason itself becomes something to ridicule, if not rejected outright. Faith alone justifies all of our acts and beliefs, just as William of Occam concluded. As Rommen explained the results of this kind of thinking,

> For Occam the natural moral law is positive law, divine will. An action is not good because of its suitableness to the essential nature of man, wherein God's archetypal idea of man is represented according to being and oughtness, but because God so wills. God's will could also have willed and decreed the precise opposite, which would then possess the same binding force as that which is now valid — which, indeed, has validity only as long as God's absolute will so determines. Law is will, pure will without any foundation in reality, without foundation in the essential nature of things. Thus, too, sin no longer contains any intrinsic element of immorality, or what is unjust, any inner element of injustice; it is an external offense against the will of God.

As a result, Occam, who sees only individual phenomena, not universals, the concepts of essences, can likewise admit no teleological orientation toward God is inherent in all creation and especially in man; or at least he cannot grant that it can be known. The unity of being, truth, and goodness does not exist for him. Moral goodness consists in mere external agreement with God's absolute will, which, subject only to His arbitrary decree, can always change. . . . Hence there exists no unchangeable *lex naturalis*, no natural law that inwardly governs the positive law. Positive law and natural law, which indeed is also positive law, stand likewise in no inner relation to each other. The identity of this thought structure with *The Prince* of Machiavelli, with the *Leviathan* of Hobbes, and with the theory of will of modern positivism (the will of the absolute sovereign is law, because no higher norm stands above him) is here quite obvious.[1]

Obviously, opinions based on faith are invalid outside of whatever group accepts those specific concepts or shares that particular interpretation of some document of faith or of revelation, or has or obtains the power to force others into compliance with what they assert must be the divine Will. (Hence the accusation so frequently heard these days that asserting any absolute standard of the good is "forcing your morality on others.") Basing the ideas of right and wrong on opinion necessarily results in the creation of a gnostic elite "inner circle" that alone is privy to the full truth that the great mass of humanity simply lacks the capacity to understand.

Legislating Morality

Thus, within this framework, it becomes the duty (or, more correctly, the delusion) of the elite to force the masses to comply with its personal interpretation as to what constitutes the good. Naturally, the means by which compliance is forced on the rest of humanity is the State, which has a monopoly on the instruments of coercion. Im-

---

[1] Rommen, *op. cit.*, 52-53.

plicitly rejecting the natural equality of all humanity — that is, that every human being by the mere fact of being human has an analogously complete capacity to acquire and develop virtue — the human race is divided into two groups. These two groups are 1) a necessarily small group of rulers — masters — and 2) the much larger group of ruled: natural slaves. Since this arrangement is presumably based on God's Will, the rulers have their positions by divine right. For their part, the ruled are under a holy obligation to obey the rulers on peril of their immortal souls . . . to say nothing of their lives, fortunes, and sacred honor. These must in all cases be sacrificed if the elite in control of the State so demand or command.

These assumptions are at the root of such productions as Sir Robert Filmer's *Patriarcha, or, The Natural Power of Kings* (1680)[2] and, of course, Thomas Hobbes's virtual manual for totalitarian government, *Leviathan, or, The Matter, Form, and Power of a Commonwealth Ecclesiastical and Civil* (1651). Within this framework, individuals have no inherent, that is, natural rights. All rights are a grant from the ruler, and are thus the result of prudential judgment on the part of the State as to what rights can be permitted, and how they are to be exercised.

The Triumph of Relativism

This extends even to the natural rights of life, liberty, pursuit of happiness (the acquisition and development of virtue), and, especially, private property. Some modern commentators, claiming to be "authentic" interpreters of, *e.g.*, the social teachings of the Catholic Church (based on the natural moral law, in common with all the major religions), have taken it on themselves to redefine the institution of private property. Often this is along the lines that private property is "a right, but not an absolute right," or is "prudential matter," and thus not, properly speaking, a natural right at all. These are meaningless statements once we understand the difference between *possessing* a right, and *exercising* a right. Nevertheless,

---

[2] *Patriarcha* was published many years after Filmer's death.

the idea that all rights come from the State is pervasive today. The idea is based on a presumption of totalitarian State power in one form or another. As Hobbes asserted,

> A Fifth doctrine, that tendeth to the Dissolution of a Common-wealth, is, *That every private man has an absolute Propriety in his Goods; such, as excludeth the Right of the Soveraign.* Every man has indeed a Propriety that excludes the Right of every other Subject: And he has it onely from the Soveraign Power; without the protection whereof, every other man should have equall Right to the same. But if the Right of the Soveraign also be excluded, he cannot performe the office they have put him into, which is, to defend them both from forraign enemies, and from the injuries of one another; and consequently there is no longer a Common-wealth.
>
> And if the Propriety of Subjects, exclude not the Right of the Soveraign Representative to their Goods; much lesse to their offices of Judicature, or Execution, in which they Represent the Soveraign himselfe.[3]

Note the subtlety of the change from the traditional understanding of the natural law. As far as Aristotle and Aquinas were concerned, every human being is a natural person. Every human being thus necessarily has those natural rights that define something as a "person."[4] How those natural rights are to be exercised, however, is a matter of prudence. That is, the exercise of a right is to be subject always to the proviso that it must never be defined in any way that effectively negates the right itself. Aristotle and Aquinas disagreed as to whether all human beings have the full — analogously complete — capacity to acquire and develop virtue, and thus the full spectrum of natural rights. The fact of natural, that is, absolute, rights, however, is not a matter of dispute.

---

[3] Thomas Hobbes, *Leviathan*, II.29.
[4] Ia IIae q. 91 a. 2.

That is, all human beings necessarily and absolutely have such natural rights as life, liberty, property, and the pursuit of happiness (the acquisition and development of virtue). They could not otherwise be defined as human beings and natural persons. It is essential to the understanding of humanity as political animals that we realize each of us has the full spectrum of natural rights, and we have *possession* of these rights absolutely — or, again, we could not be defined as "human persons."

No Right is Absolute in Its Exercise

No one, however, has or could possibly have the absolute *exercise* of any right, even a natural right. That is impossible in any event, given humanity's social nature. No right can be exercised except within the confines of the common good. This in turn precludes the exercise of any right in any way that harms the right holder, other persons, or the common good. You cannot legitimately violate anyone's rights by the exercise of your own rights. As John Locke pointed out, you are not even "allowed" to violate your own rights, *e.g.*, by voluntarily selling yourself into slavery or committing suicide.[5] That would imply that your presumably inalienable rights to life and liberty are, in fact, alienable. If you can alienate your own rights, even with your own full and free consent, what is to stop others from alienating your rights without your consent once the precedent of alienation has been established?

Ultimately, the claim that a ruler holds his or her position by some kind of divine right, that is, either by a direct grant of authority from God or some other Power, or believes it to be self-generated or unaccountable, is a claim to divine status. Thus, by claiming that ordinary people do not have absolute possession of their natural rights — in effect, that natural rights are not, in fact, rights at all, but "prudential matter" — the State (or the ruler who claims to personify the State, especially by his or her own authority) usurps the place of God.

---

[5] John Locke, *First Treatise of Government*, § 42.

Understood in this way, basing the natural law on the Will rather than the Intellect is clearly contrary to reason — and, possibly, one of the reasons why Aquinas declared that the law is discernible by reason alone.[6] Basing the natural law on the Will is one of those seemingly "small errors" in the beginning that lead to big errors in the end, as both Aristotle and Aquinas pointed out. Nowhere is this more evident than in how we relate to the institutions of the social order, those props intended and presumably designed to assist each individual in the task of acquiring and developing virtue, and thereby becoming more fully human.

Sovereignty, Money, and Credit

The particular great error on which we will now focus is the idea that the State is or can be sovereign in and of itself, or by direct grant of Heaven, without reference to the individual sovereignty of the human person under God.

The idea that the State is somehow sovereign in and of itself or has been granted some kind of sovereignty directly by God leads inevitably to the belief that all rights come not directly from God to natural persons as part of nature itself, but from the State or the collective to individuals as a revocable grant. The individual is resumed to be utterly helpless in any social situation, unless he or she is directly assisted by the State. This assistance inevitably takes the form of direct control over the life, liberty, property, and acquisition and development of virtue of each citizen. Every individual becomes a "mere creature of the State," existing as a person only at the sufferance and permission of the State, which thereby becomes all-powerful.

Nowhere is this more immediately evident than in the institutions of money and credit, the life's blood, so to speak, of the body politic. As the 19th century economist Charles Morrison explained,

---

[6] Ia IIae, q. 90, a. 1.

Confidence and credit are only moral elements in society; they may be said to be, to a great extent, mere matters of opinion; yet their importance in the production and distribution of wealth is so great, that the whole machinery of material production is kept at work, disordered, or paralyzed, according as these principles act in a healthy manner, irregularly, or not at all. They are to our industrial community what the nervous system is to the body, a slight and sensitive substance in itself, but the indispensable cause of all the life and motion of the system. A great nation may possess in abundance all the means of producing wealth, — population, intelligence, capital, natural and artificial instruments of production; and yet, if credit and confidence should be from any cause destroyed, all these resources seem to have lost their virtue, and general distress prevails. Let confidence and credit be restored, and the whole system is immediately set in motion again, and in a very short time general prosperity returns.[7]

Money and credit, as the economist Irving Fisher explained,[8] are based on private property. Credit, simply put, is delivering something of value to another conditional upon the future return of something of equal value. Extending credit creates a debt. Money is whatever is used to convey value to a creditor; it consists of anything that is or can be accepted in settlement of a debt. Money is not created by a *command* from the issuer, but by an *offer*, the acceptance of which constitutes a contract, and thereby creates money.

Money and Private Property

Money is thus always something that conveys a property right in the present value of existing or future market-

---

[7] Charles Morrison, *An Essay on the Relations Between Labour and Capital*. London: Longman, Brown, Green, and Longmans, 1854, 200.

[8] Irving Fisher, *The Purchasing Power of Money*. New York: Macmillan, 1931, 4.

able goods and services. This, obviously, implies that whoever or whatever makes an offer to convey a property right *has* a property right in those marketable goods and services to convey; that he, she, or it "owns" whatever backs the offer, or has a legal claim on the thing of value sufficient to derive and issue claims against the thing of value. Making an offer backed by something that the issuer does not own or to which he or she does not have a legal claim is theft, a violation of private property; the issuer is making promises for someone else to keep, or is committing theft in some other fashion.

By understanding money and credit as the medium of exchange of the present value of existing or future marketable goods and services belonging to the issuer — that is, anything that can be accepted in settlement of a debt — anyone can participate in the economic process and engage in exchange simply by establishing his or her "credit" in the community. That is, someone demonstrates to the satisfaction of all parties to any transaction in which the one seeking to establish credit participates that he or she will make good on his or her promise to deliver value on demand or at some agreed-upon future date or on the occurrence of some event. The ability to enter into a contract is an inherent aspect of individual human sovereignty, coming under freedom of association (liberty), and is based on private property. Every person is (or should be) free to enter into a contract (free association) to deliver value immediately or in the future (private property), and to have that offer accepted, thereby creating money.

Part of this explanation might confuse some people. They may wonder how or why the power to deliver value immediately or in the future comes under "private property." This confusion is easily cleared up once we understand that "property" does not refer to the thing that is owned, but to the inalienable (absolute) right to be an owner that every human being has, and to the socially determined bundle of rights that define how an owner may use what he or she owns. "Property," as the late lawyer-economist Louis O. Kelso pointed out, in everyday speech connotes "control." Thus, the power to deliver something of value immediately or in the future signifies the owner's exercise of control in the form of the right of disposal over what he or she owns — private property.

Say's Law of Markets

Logically, anyone who wishes to participate in the economy must have the means to do so. This, in turn, means that everyone who wishes to participate in the economy must have ownership of something, whether labor or capital, preferably both. Further, that ownership must be exclusive, that is, the owner must have the right to exclude others from the use and enjoyment of that which he or she owns.

There are circumstances that justify limiting or even confiscating a portion of what someone owns for the common good, but only to the extent that 1) it is absolutely necessary and no other recourse is possible, 2) the owner is justly compensated in some fashion, and 3) the owner's right to be an owner is in no way limited or abolished.

Only by connecting money directly to private property can the process of money creation be carried out legitimately. This is because unless we have something of value to back our promises, we cannot make good promises. The economy will not function, just as Charles Morrison pointed out. As Jean-Baptiste Say explained,

> Since the time of Adam Smith, political economists have agreed that we do not in reality buy the objects we consume, with the money or circulating coin which we pay for them. We must in the first place have bought this money itself by the sale of productions of our own. To the proprietor of the mines whence this money is obtained, it is a production with which he purchases such commodities as he may have occasion for: to all those into whose hands this money afterwards passes, it is only the price of the productions which they have themselves created by means of their lands, capital, or industry. In selling these, they ex-

change first their productions for money; and they afterwards exchange this money for objects of consumption. It is then in strict reality with their productions that they make their purchases; it is impossible for them to buy any articles whatever to a greater amount than that which they have produced either by themselves, or by means of their capitals and lands.[9]

The "job" of money is thus to facilitate participation in the economic process. If people need this thing called "money," they produce a good or service to offer in exchange for the goods and services produced by others and, by the acceptance of that offer create money by means of a contract backed by the promise to redeem the money in the future, or borrow existing money on the strength of their promise to produce a good or service in the future to repay the loan. Obviously, common sense tells us that if we borrow money, we should only do so if that on which we spend the money produces something that we can use to repay the loan. We are otherwise diminishing our future ability to meet our consumption needs out of our own resources — in effect, robbing not only Peter, but ourselves to repay Paul.

If we reflect on Say's explanation of the role of this thing we call "money," we come to a number of conclusions. The most important of these is that anyone can create money simply by having "good credit" and by exercising his or her right of free association to enter into contracts with others. The actual thing or things that two parties to a transaction agree to exchange between themselves are irrelevant to anybody who is not a party to the transaction. It can — and has been — such things as stamped lumps of gold, silver, and bronze, cattle, tobacco, playing cards, wooden tokens, promissory notes, even elephants or human skulls. All that is necessary is that someone either have a good or service that he or she has

---

[9] Jean-Baptiste Say, *Letters to Mr. Malthus on Several Subjects of Political Economy and on the Cause of the Stagnation of Commerce*. London: Sherwood, Neely & Jones, 1821, 2.

produced, or be reasonably certain that a good or service can be produced in the future so that it is available for delivery when the "money" is redeemed, thereby making good on the promise. As Say further explained to Malthus,

> From these premises I had drawn a conclusion which appeared to me evident, but which seems to have startled you. I had said, "As each of us can only purchase the productions of others with his own productions — as the value we can buy is equal to the value we can produce, the more men can produce, the more they will purchase." Thence follows the other conclusion, which you refuse to admit: "that if certain goods remain unsold, it is because other goods are not produced; and that it is production alone which opens markets to produce."[10]

This is "Say's Law of Markets." To summarize as briefly as possible, production equals income; supply generates its own demand, and demand, its own supply — in aggregate, of course.

Unfortunately, while this understanding of money is both logical and derived directly from the common sense precepts of the natural moral law based on the Intellect and discerned through the use of reason, it is neither widely understood nor accepted today.[11]

Instead, the world has been saddled with an understanding of money accepted as a virtual religious dogma based on an approach derived from positivism, an almost pure moral relativism, that is, the Will, rather than the Intellect. We will examine the approach to money and credit based on the Will in the next chapter.

---

[10] *Ibid.*, 3.

[11] For an analysis of the effect of changes in the money supply linked directly to the present value of existing and future marketable goods and services, *vide* Norman G. Kurland, "A New Look at Prices and Money: The Kelsonian Binary Model for Achieving Rapid Growth Without Inflation," *The Journal of Socio-Economics*, Vol. 30, 495-515.

6. Re-Editing the Dictionary

In the previous chapter we looked at an understanding of money and credit based on an approach to the natural moral law derived from the Intellect and discerned by reason, rather than from the Will and accepted on faith. We saw that this understanding of money was summarized by the late 18th, early 19th century political economist Jean-Baptiste Say. This "Say's Law of Markets" can briefly be stated as "production equals income." Thus, in the aggregate, "supply generates its own demand, and demand its own supply."

A Different Definition of Money

Unfortunately, there is another understanding of money and credit. This is one that has become accepted as economic orthodoxy, despite the fact that it contradicts both common sense and sound philosophy, to say nothing of the natural moral law. Nor was Say unaware that there were economists and others (notably Malthus) who disagreed with his analysis. As Say explained,

> I am aware that this proposition has a paradoxical appearance, which creates prejudices against it; I know that common prejudices are more likely to support the opinions of those who maintain that there is too much produce, because every body is engaged in creating it: that instead of constantly producing, we ought to increase unproductive consumption, and devour our old capitals instead of accumulating new ones. This doctrine has indeed appearances on its side: it may be supported by arguments; and may interpret facts in its favour. But, Sir, when Copernicus and Galileo first taught that the sun (although it was daily seen to rise in the east, ascend majestically to the meridian, and decline at evening in the west) never moved from its station, they also had to contend

with universal prejudice, the opinion of antiquity, the evidence of the senses: ought they to have renounced the demonstrations resulting from sound philosophy? I should wrong you, were I to doubt of your answer.[1]

The crux of the issue, and the basis for the misunderstanding between Say and Malthus, is that each used a different definition (and thus understanding) of "money." As we might expect, these different definitions of a concept as fundamental as money have been evocative of much confusion about the science of political economy, particularly where it overlaps into the moral philosophy, which necessarily provides the foundation of all the social sciences.

To Say, "money" is anything that can be accepted in settlement of a debt. As previously noted, this includes anything and everything that people use as a medium of exchange of a property right in the present value of existing or future marketable goods and services. This is the case whether or not a third party has put some kind of stamp of approval on it. This is, essentially, the basic principle of the "British Banking School." As long as something can be accepted in settlement of a debt in a free exchange, it counts as "money," regardless who issued it, or even what it is.

To Malthus and those who take the position at odds with that of the Banking School, "money" is limited to that which is recognized by the State as the official medium of exchange. To be legitimate, it must have the sanction of the State. No transaction is legitimate unless it is carried out by means of whatever the State has authorized to be used as money, and with the explicit approval of the State.

The reason for giving the State this much power is that in this understanding, "money" is a claim not on the assets of the issuer, but on those of society at large; the issuer becomes *de facto* owner of everything. "Money" shifts

---

[1] *Letters to Mr. Malthus, op. cit.,* 3.

from something that is accepted in settlement of a debt, that is, an offer and acceptance (contract), to a command, an exercise of property on the part of the issuer not in his own assets, but in the assets belonging to others. This effectively abolishes private property.

The State is God

This is the basic principle of the British Currency School. It assumes a State so powerful that, like a god, it can presumably command changes in the natural law itself. The State does this by claiming the right to define not just the *exercise* of rights, but the *substance* of rights, the very essence of reality. Perhaps John Maynard Keynes, the chief architect of modern economics, described it best in his *Treatise on Money*:

> It is a peculiar characteristic of money contracts that it is the State or Community not only which enforces delivery, but also which decides what it is that must be delivered as a lawful or customary discharge of a contract which has been concluded in terms of the money-of-account. The State, therefore, comes in first of all as the authority of law which enforces the payment of the thing which corresponds to the name or description in the contract. But it comes in doubly when, in addition, it claims the right to determine and declare *what thing* corresponds to the name, and to vary its declaration from time to time — when, that is to say, it claims the right to re-edit the dictionary. This right is claimed by all modern States and has been so claimed for some four thousand years at least. It is when this stage in the evolution of Money has been reached that Knapp's Chartalism — the doctrine that money is peculiarly a creation of the State — is fully realized.[2]

---

[2] John Maynard Keynes, *A Treatise on Money, Volume I: The Pure Theory of Money*. New York: Harcourt, Brace and Company, 1930, 4.

According to Keynes, then, the State is effectively God — for nothing other than a Supreme Being has or could have the power to redefine the substantial nature of a thing, and thereby transubstantiate one thing into another. Keynes claimed for the State as something ordinary the extraordinary ability to change reality itself: "the right to re-edit the dictionary"! We can only pause in wonder, even awe, at the ready and unquestioning acceptance of such a claim and statement on the part of the State in the realms of political science and economics.

According to Keynes, then, "money" is not an offer, *i.e.*, of anything that can be accepted in settlement of a debt. Instead, money is a purchase order issued by the State, or by a State-sanctioned individual or organization. Just as Hobbes claimed in *Leviathan*, the State is presumed to be the ultimate owner of everything. Nothing except official State issues can be used as the medium of exchange; by no other means can contracts be entered into or fulfilled. Freedom of association is abolished, and even the substantial nature of reality has been altered — presumably.

The Problem with Keynes

Keynes's explanation, however, while superficially plausible once you accept the idea of divine right or an all-powerful State (and, in fact, reflects what many people today firmly and sincerely believe), is completely wrong. It is a declaration of pure legal and moral positivism, the sort of thinking that the noted German jurist Heinrich Rommen declared leads ultimately to nihilism, and to which he traced the rise of Nazism. Contrary to the statement that such absolutism has been "claimed by all modern States and . . . so claimed for some four thousand years at least," Keynes's belief and faith in absolute State power is (as we have seen already in this book) actually of relatively recent appearance on the political stage — and is not, in any event, "claimed by all modern States." Contrary to Keynes's declaration, the United States of America explicitly vests sovereignty not in the State, but in "We, the People."

Ultimately, the issue boils down to nothing more than the Medieval argument as to whether God's Intellect (Nature/Reason) has the primacy, or whether God's — or the State's — revealed Will is supreme. We can easily see, then, that Keynes's concept of "money" is directly contrary to the Thomist understanding of the natural moral law. It assumes as a given that "law is will" (*lex voluntas*) instead of "law is reason" (*lex ratio*).[3] In Keynes's and the Currency School's positivist orientation, money, like law, is whatever the State says it is. This is claimed to be so, regardless of the underlying principle, whether it be actual value represented, or the dictates of justice as discerned by reason, respectively. As Rommen explained,

> Natural law is the consequence of the doctrines of the priority of the intellect over the will (law is reason) in both God and man, of the knowability of the essences of things and their essential order, their metaphysical being and the ordered hierarchy of values. Positivism, on the other hand, is the consequence of the doctrine of the primacy of the will with respect to the intellect in both theology and human psychology. Besides, *voluntas* here means more than mere will: it denotes passion, irrational appetite, and so on. Positivism signifies the renouncing of all efforts to know the essences of things (nominalism), the repudiation of the metaphysics of hierarchized being and value. Accordingly it is also found in the same conceptual pattern in the things of the nineteenth and twentieth centuries, even though it is concealed under different names.[4]

The idea that money is anything that can be accepted in settlement of a debt is consistent with the understanding of the natural law based on reason (*lex ratio*), while the belief that money is and can only be what the State declares to be money is an application of pure moral positivism, indeed, even tyranny.

---

[3] Rommen, *op. cit.*, 36.
[4] *Ibid.*

Might Makes Right

Modern political absolutism, such as Keynes erroneous-
ly declared has been around for "some four thousand
years," is rooted in the theories of "divine right." This followed hard on the heels of the Reformation, as John Neville Figgis noted. The growth of the idea that the natural
moral law is based not on the Intellect, but on the Will,
that is, personal opinion and (ultimately) Kallikles the
Sophist's dictum that "might makes right."

As we saw, this school of thought reached its highest
(or, depending on your point of view, its lowest) development in Stuart England with the totalitarian political philosophies of Sir Robert Filmer and Thomas Hobbes.[5] Far
from being unchallenged and pervasive for thousands of
years as Keynes claimed, State absolutism was countered
by political philosophies at least as far back as Aristotle in
The Nichomachean Ethics, The Politics and *The Athenian
Constitution*, and Aquinas in *De Regimine Principum* and
the treatise on law in the *Summa*.

Not that any refutation of the mania for legal and moral
positivism and State absolutism has made any difference
in the modern world. Many people today are absolutely
convinced that the State is the sole means of effecting
changes in the common good, even in reality itself. Aristotle's idea persists that the individual is helpless in the
face of existing social structures or conditions. Only a divinely instituted State or one that exists on its own authority (so modern political scientists and economists assume) has the power to act on the common good, and that
only indirectly.

The implications of the claim that the State alone has
the power to define what people can use as money (and
who can use it) are thus, to put it mildly, breathtaking.

---

[5] A good, if somewhat incomplete review of 17th century political
theory that unfortunately misstates and denigrates non-English
thinkers, is David Wooten, ed., *Divine Right and Democracy: An
Anthology of Political Writing in Stuart England*. London: Penguin Books, 1986.

This has led to the situation so ably described by Pope Pius XI in his landmark encyclical, *Quadragesimo Anno*, "On the Restructuring of the Social Order," issued in 1931. As Pius XI observed,

> In the first place, it is obvious that not only is wealth concentrated in our times but an immense power and despotic economic dictatorship is consolidated in the hands of a few, who often are not owners but only the trustees and managing directors of invested funds which they administer according to their own arbitrary will and pleasure.

> This dictatorship is being most forcibly exercised by those who, since they hold the money and completely control it, control credit also and rule the lending of money. Hence they regulate the flow, so to speak, of the life-blood whereby the entire economic system lives, and have so firmly in their grasp the soul, as it were, of economic life that no one can breathe against their will.[6]

Although Keynes's view of money and the role of the State is admittedly the prevailing view in the modern world, it did not (despite Keynes's claim that it had developed out of the accepted theory of State absolutism for "four thousand years") go unchallenged. Aquinas opposed the theory after it made its first appearance in the 12th century. In the 16th century, when the belief that the natural moral law is based on the Will rather than the Intellect gained new momentum from the Reformation, the argument in support of the Intellect was strengthened, notably through the work of Cardinal Bellarmine.

The New Heterodoxy

After the Reformation, the "right" political theory that went along with the new views on religion was *divine* right. This fit in perfectly with the new idea of the State that developed as the Middle Ages faded. The head of

---

[6] Pius XI, *Quadragesimo Anno* ("On the Restructuring of the Social Order"), 1931, §§ 105-106.

State was now also considered the head of the local church, holding both positions by heavenly fiat. In support of the new absolutist concept of the State, political scientists claimed that ordinary people were made solely to serve God by serving the State and its divinely appointed head. Man was made for the State, not the State for man. The democratic ideal inherited from Rome that underpinned Medieval political theory was completely overthrown.

The innovation of divine right was one of many "new things" that came out of a rejection of Aristotelian philosophy and Thomism. It was perhaps best stated by Sir Robert Filmer, the chief theologian of James I of England (James VI of Scotland), in *Patriarcha, or, The Natural Power of Kings*, written in the mid-17th century, but not published until 1680, after Filmer's death. As Filmer proclaimed in the first sentence of his work,

> Since the time that school divinity began to flourish there hath been a common opinion maintained, as well by divines as by divers other learned men, which affirms:
>
>> "Mankind is naturally endowed and born with freedom from all subjection, and at liberty to choose what form of government it please, and that the power which any one man hath over others was at first bestowed according to the discretion of the multitude."
>
> This tenet was first hatched in the schools, and hath been fostered by all succeeding Papists.[7]

Filmer then spent the rest of his short work ridiculing the idea of the sovereignty of the individual under God. He also made arguments that later political scientists, such as John Locke and Algernon Sidney, were able to shred, more or less with ease, through the application of a modicum of common sense.

---

[7] Robert Filmer, *Patriarcha, or, The Natural Power of Kings*, I.

CHAPTER 6 55

A Learned Doctor

Locke and Sidney, however (like *Patriarcha*), came some time after Filmer's death. During Filmer's lifetime, his chief adversary was a cardinal of the Roman Curia from the obscure Italian mountain village of Montepulciano. This was Robert Bellarmine, possibly one of the most learned men of his age. (He taught himself Hebrew in a matter of weeks, and composed a grammar for that language that was used for generations.[8])

Bellarmine was so effective an adversary of the new theories in politics and religion a rumor spread that "Robert Bellarmine" was actually the pseudonym of a group of highly trained scholars. As John Clement Rager recounts,

> The learned Englishman Whitaker (d. 1595) said: "Until now we were ignorant of the true position of the Roman Church. Since Bellarmine has come forward we know exactly what that Church teaches upon every article of faith." Some were unwilling to believe that one man could have been the author of so voluminous and powerful a work. They began to suspect that under the name "Robert Bellarmine" was concealed the whole army of Jesuit theologians. Robert, they said, stood for "robur" — strength; Bellarmine, for "belle" — wars, "arma" — weapons, "minae" — threats.[9]

An amusing anecdote, but more to the point, though, how did Bellarmine counter the newly arisen divine right of kings theory of political sovereignty?

Bellarmine wrote extensively on the source, transmission, and application of the civil power, that is, of political sovereignty. In *De Laicis, or, The Treatise on Civil Government,* written to oppose the Protestant doctrine of the

[8] James Brodrick, S.J., *Robert Bellarmine: Saint and Scholar.* Westminster, UK: The Newman Press, 1961, 44-46.
[9] John Clement Rager, *The Political Philosophy of St. Robert Bellarmine.* Spokane, Washington: The Apostolate of Our Lady of Siluva, 1995, 14.

"Divine Right of Kings" and defend the legitimacy of civil authority, Bellarmine presented the case for government of the people, by the people, and for the people.

Taking his arguments and proofs from Scripture, the examples of the saints, from purpose or necessity, from considerations of the efficient cause, and from considerations of the source of secular power, Bellarmine declared that the legitimacy of political power is demonstrated by the fact that it is necessary, man being social. Civil government would thus be legitimate even if the sin of Adam had never occurred: "For even if servile subjection began after the sin of Adam, nevertheless there would have been political government even while man was in the state of innocence. And this is proved, firstly, because even then man would have been by nature a political and social animal, and hence would have had need of a ruler."[10] (Note Bellarmine's distinction between *political* and *social*.)

This power is not, according to Bellarmine, vested in a particular ruler or class, but in the people as a whole. This is a dangerous concept, and one that Pius XI later had to correct, reminding us that God only grants rights directly to "natural persons." Artificial persons such as the State can only receive rights by delegation or "reflection" from from God by way of natural persons.

Bellarmine evidently failed to remember that the "collected body" of the people is as artificial as the State itself. An excuse for making such an egregious error may have been that Bellarmine was addressing the issue of whether God grants the ruler power directly, or whether this power is a grant from the people. The dangerous insertion of the collective was something he might have passed over as not something relating to the issue at hand. As Bellarmine explained,

> Political power considered in general, not descending in particular to Monarchy, Aristocracy, or Democracy, comes directly from God alone; for this follows of ne-

---

[10] *De Laicis*, Ch. VII.

cessity from the nature of man, since that nature comes from Him Who made it; besides, this power derives from the natural law, since it does not depend upon the consent of men; for, willing or unwilling, they must be ruled over by some one, unless they wish the human race to perish. . . .

Note, secondly, that this power resides, as in its subject, immediately in the whole State, for this power is by Divine law, but Divine law gives this power to no particular man, therefore Divine law gives this power to the collected body. Furthermore, in the absence of positive law, there is no good reason why, in a multitude of equals, one rather than another should dominate. Therefore, power belongs to the collected body.[11]

Yes, this inserts the collective between the government and the individual people. Whether we posit the existence of the collective, or whether we assume that political power is transmitted directly from God through the individuals who make up the nation, however, makes no essential difference to the point Bellarmine was making: that political power — political sovereignty — comes to the ruler not directly from God, but from God through the people, and that the ruler only governs with their consent.

Still, Bellarmine left us with the dangerous idea of the collective inserted between God and man. As Pope Pius XI reminded the world a few centuries later, "Only man, the human person, and not society in any form, is endowed with reason and a morally free will."[12] In the next chapter we will look at how later political scientists, particularly John Locke and Algernon Sidney, tried to get around this problem.

---

[11] *Ibid.*, Ch. VI.
[12] Pius XI, *Divini Redemptoris* ("On Atheistic Communism"), 1937, § 29.

7. The State of Nature

In the previous chapter we saw that Cardinal Bellarmine refuted the theory of divine right of kings. Bellarmine defended the essence of democracy: that sovereignty resides primarily in the people, who then grant a portion of it to their chosen ruler or rulers. This was just as Aquinas had claimed a few centuries previously in *De Regimine Principum*. Bellarmine reaffirmed the essential tenet of Scholastic philosophy that in civil society God grants sovereignty exclusively to natural persons, not to offices, that is, individuals in their "official capacities."

The Law of Contradiction

Unfortunately, Bellarmine's analysis assumed that there are certain rights that, unlike life, liberty, and private property, are granted not to individual human beings, but to the collective, the "assembled mass" of the people. These include such rights as waging war or administering justice. The collective, however, is not a natural person. God therefore cannot by Nature — Intellect — grant the collective any kind of right or rights. As Pope Pius XI reminded us, "Only man, the human person, and not society in any form, is endowed with reason and a morally free will."[1]

This raises the issue as to whether God could not chose, if He so desired, to violate His own rules, and decide to grant sovereignty directly to the State or a ruler as a ruler. That is, is there anything God cannot do?

The answer to that question is, "Yes: not be God." By definition, as a perfect Being, God cannot contradict Himself, or He would not be God. Thus He cannot do anything contrary to His own Nature — such as endow anything that is not a natural person (such as the collective) with

---

[1] *Divini Redemptoris, op. cit.*, § 29.

inherent rights, for that is contrary to what it means for something to be a natural person reflecting God's Nature.

Thus, what "saves" Bellarmine from Hobbesian State absolutism is a firm reliance on the primacy of the Intellect over the Will as the basis of the natural law, as Rommen pointed out.[2] If God (or the State) appears to give a command or passes a law that seems to contradict Nature, we are either misunderstanding God's command, or the State may be acting beyond its competence, respectively. It is our job as faithful creatures or good citizens to discern the underlying reality or principle in conformity with Nature, and apply it properly. The State or ruler cannot, therefore, be supreme in the way that Hobbes or Filmer declared. This is because State absolutism is itself contrary to the law of Nature and of Nature's God, violating the sovereignty of the individual and the dignity of the human person.

Can Things Have Inherent Rights?

The necessity of the collective for Bellarmine's argument comes from his assumption that the State or the ruler (both "artificial persons") have legitimate powers that individuals lack, such as carrying out a just war or judging criminals. He did not consider the possibility of what Pope Pius XI was to discover and at which Aquinas hinted: that individuals have certain rights that they cannot exercise *as individuals*. Bellarmine assumed the necessity of the collective because he rejected the possibility of what John Locke, for example, referred to as "the state of nature," wherein there was absolutely no civil society because there was no civil intercourse. Bellarmine looked on this assumption as purely imaginary, and unworthy of consideration. From the creation of Adam, man has lived in social intercourse with his fellows ("It is not good for the man to be alone."[3]). Civil society, therefore, existed the moment there was more than one person.

---

[2] Rommen, *op. cit.*, 53.
[3] Genesis, 2:18.

...the statement is false which Cicero makes, namely, that there was formerly a time when men wandered about in the manner of beasts, then, through the eloquence of some wise orator, they were induced to assemble, and to live together.[4] Indeed, whoever undertakes the praise of eloquence usually makes this statement even now. But that state of affairs never existed, nor could it have existed at any time. For Adam was a very wise man, and without doubt did not allow men to wander about like beasts, and Cain, his son, even built a material city; before Cain and Adam, man did not exist.[5]

Locke, however, while in most cases following Bellarmine's arguments closely (at the same time that he claimed to be rejecting them — it is complicated), had no problem with positing a time in which men had no social intercourse with one another. There was, therefore, a time when each individual person retained both full individual sovereignty and full political sovereignty within himself.

For our purposes, let us assume for the sake of the argument that the state of nature would be a purely hypothetical situation. This would be similar to slavery, which, while Locke refused to admit that anyone could be a slave legitimately — i.e., completely deprived of rights — the notion of slavery was a useful concept, and was, at least, intellectually conceivable, even if absolutely impossible. *Hypothetically*, then, a state of nature could exist antecedent to the existence of civil society, where only one person was around, with no one else within his sphere, even if that state of nature disappeared instantaneously with that individual's creation due to the existence of others within his sphere.

Where that single individual was all alone, he would be a completely independent and politically sovereign entity. This assumption, added to the additional assumption that man retains full individual and political sovereignty in

---

[4] Cicero, *De Inventione*, Book I.
[5] *De Laicis*, Ch. V.

each person, even with others around, is the basis for anarchy as a political system (as distinct from mere social chaos). Bellarmine (and probably Locke as well) would have denied the possibility that genuine anarchy could exist where there was more than one person. This is because the existence of society obviates the possibility of anarchy, and society exists immediately where there is more than one person.

Rights Require Others

The theory is that the moment another human being shows up, a society exists, and an individual loses those rights of political sovereignty that he formerly had, of carrying out a just war, or judging the guilty, for example. You thus have the paradox where man in the state of nature has full political sovereignty, but only as long as he does not have the opportunity of exercising it. That is, there is no one else around against whom to exercise the rights exclusive to political sovereignty.

Individuals, the moment they enter society (whether or not that action is voluntary or even conscious), commit by that action an automatic grant of their political sovereignty to duly constituted authority. Since society exists the moment there is more than one person, the "state of nature" can be taken as completely and purely hypothetical, a useful fiction for determining the method of transmission of political sovereignty.

Locke probably did not seriously consider the possibility of anarchy ("the state of nature") as an actual state of affairs, and probably would have looked on today's anarchists as lunatics. In common with Bellarmine and virtually every other thinker throughout history, Locke viewed man as a social creature, whose interaction with his fellows as beings with something in common with himself was the only rational arrangement. The insertion of a period in which a state of nature existed was for Locke probably only a useful contrivance.

Our assumption of a hypothetical state of nature, however, is also extremely useful in getting around Bellarmine's difficulty about the State or the collective having rights that individuals lack. Bellarmine assumed the existence of society from the very creation of man. We can assume the hypothetical existence of a state of nature that disappeared immediately upon the first instance of social interaction. This, as far as Bellarmine was concerned, was virtually instantaneous, making the actual existence of the "state of nature" impossible, however useful Locke found it in deriving arguments.

Thus, for the sake of the argument and to get around the difficulties posed by Cardinal Bellarmine's insertion of the collective between God and man, and between man and the State, we can assume the existence of a "state of nature." This would remove, at least in part, the presumed necessity of the existence of rights that God grants to something that is not a natural person. As Locke explains in his *Second Treatise on Government*,

> Wherever, therefore, any number of men so unite into one society, as to quit every one his executive power of the law of nature, and to resign it to the public, there, and there only, is a political, or civil society. And this is done wherever any number of men, in the state of nature, enter into society to make one people one body politic, under one supreme government, or else when any one joins himself to, and incorporates with, any government already made. For hereby he authorizes the society, or, which is all one, the legislative thereof, to make laws for him, as the public good of the society shall require, to the execution whereof his own assistance (as to his own decrees) is due. And this puts men out of a state of nature into that of a commonwealth.[6]

Consent of the Governed

Where the ruler or group charged with the rule is carrying out its mandate to conform to the natural moral law and promote the common good, we have to assume that

---

[6] John Locke, *Second Treatise on Government,* § 89

the consent of the governed, after the initial establishment, has been given automatically. No single individuals or groups, acting on their own authority, can decide that the current government is illegitimate, and work for its overthrow or go into rebellion. This would be a criminal act, contrary to the common good.

When, however, the government is engaged in egregious violation of the natural moral law, or is acting directly contrary to the common good in an obvious and material fashion, there may then be just cause to revoke the grant of political sovereignty made to the present government, and vest it in another group or form of government. As Aquinas explained, "If any society of people have the right of choosing a king for itself, it is not unjust if he be deposed by the same, or if his power be curbed, when by a royal tyranny he abuses his power."[7] This was echoed by John Locke in the 19th chapter of his *Second Treatise on Civil Government*, "There is therefore secondly another way whereby governments are dissolved, and that is when the legislative or the prince, either of them, act contrary to their trust." As Locke continued,

> First, the legislative acts against the trust reposed in them when they endeavour to invade the property of the subject, and to make themselves or any part of the community masters or arbitrary disposers of the lives, liberties, or fortunes of the people. . . .What I have said here concerning the legislative in general, holds true also concerning the supreme executor, who having a double trust put in him, both to have a part in the legislative and the supreme execution of the law, acts against both when he goes about to set up his own arbitrary will as the law of the society. He acts also contrary to his trust when he either employs the force, treasure, and offices of the society, to corrupt the representatives, and gain them to his purposes; or openly pre-engages the electors, and prescribes to

---

[7] *De Regimine Principum* ("On the Rule of Princes"), Book I, Chapter vi.

their choice such whom he has by solicitations,
threats, promises, or otherwise won to his designs,
and employs them to bring in such, who have prom-
ised beforehand what to vote and what to enact.[8]

Anyone familiar with the Declaration of Independence
of the United States, as well as the Virginia Declaration
of Rights, adopted nearly a month earlier, will recognize
the basis and justification of the English colonies in America joining together and repudiating the governance of the
King of Great Britain by revoking the grant of sovereignty:

Whenever any form of government becomes destructive of these ends, it is the Right of the People to alter
or abolish it, and to institute a new government. . .
.Prudence, indeed, will dictate that governments long
established should not be changed for light and tran-
sient causes.[9]

A Change in Government

What are the conditions that justify a change in government? First, oppression must be habitual, tyrannical,
and intolerable. Second, other remedies must have failed;
legal and peaceful means must have been ineffective.
Third, there must be reasonable probability of success. As
Aquinas pointed out, "If indeed a tyranny is not excessive,
it is better to bear it for a time, than, by acting against
the tyrant, to be involved in many perils, which are worse
than tyranny. For it may happen that they who rise
against a tyrant do not prevail against him; and so the
tyrant, being incensed, rages the more violently."[10]

---

[8] *Second Treatise on Government*, §§ 221-222.
[9] *Vide* the Virginia Declaration of Rights, June 12, 1776, "When
government fails to confer common benefit, a majority of the
people have a right to change it." Also Bellarmine, *De Laicis*, Ch.
VI, "For legitimate reason [the people] can change the government to an aristocracy or a democracy or *vice versa*. . . . It depends upon the consent of men to place over themselves a king,
consul, or magistrate."
[10] *De Regimine Principum*, Book I., Ch. vi.

Fourth, and finally, the revolt ought to be approved by the majority and by the best men of the land.

Although the work of Bellarmine, Locke, and Sidney in some measure discredited divine right theory, it left two problems in place. One, Bellarmine, due to his insertion of the collective, inadvertently gave ultimate power to the State — although that was clearly not his intention. Within this framework, the State (as Father Heinrich Pesch, S.J., was to note later) is presumed to be the mediate, that is, the indirect cause of individual welfare. This is chiefly through the State's care of the general welfare. In extraordinary cases, however, and on a temporary basis, the State is justified taking over direct care of individual welfare.

In the nature of things, however, the State inevitably moves to take over control of as much of everything as possible by becoming the *immediate* cause of individual welfare. To paraphrase the old saying, give the State an inch, and it will take a mile. All rights, even life, liberty, and property, become interpreted as "prudential matter," to be exercised or even granted solely at the discretion of the State. As far as the bottom line goes, this was not an improvement over basing the natural moral law on the Will — and falls into the "law is will" camp by default.

Two, if we go the other way and base our understanding of sovereignty on the "state of nature" argument, we secure recognition of humanity's individual inalienable natural (that is, absolute) rights, but we tend to lose sight of the fact that no right is or can be absolute in its exercise. The nature of the human person and of society itself demands that the exercise of all rights be defined in a way that not only respects the human dignity of the individual right holder, but of all other individuals in society, groups, and, of course, the common good itself. Unfortunately, when we base our argument on the assumption of a state of nature, we tend to define possession of natural rights correctly as absolute, but also (and incorrectly) include the exercise of rights as absolute as well.

Thus, by claiming that all rights come from the State, the collectivist puts the State in the place of God. By claiming absolute exercise of rights, the individualist usurps the place of God.

The situation was not, however, hopeless. It was only confused. We will start to look at how these problems were resolved in the next chapter.

8. A New World

In the previous chapter, we discovered that, regardless which political theory we adopt, we seem to fall into one of two traps, individualism or collectivism. Both are unacceptable. If we admit humanity's social nature, we evidently have to accept that the State or the collective, something that is not a natural person, can somehow receive a grant of rights directly from God, or itself be God. Ultimately, this denies the sovereignty of the human person under God.

If, on the other hand, we recognize humanity's individual nature, then the State itself (an artifact that, while man-made like other tools, is natural and essential to human development), seems to acquire a degree of illegitimacy, if only by serving as the agency by means of which what would otherwise be the absolute exercise of our natural rights is limited.

A Third Way

While Europe was struggling between the Scylla and Charybdis of individualism and collectivism, however, something new was growing up in the New World — or perhaps it would be more accurate to say that an ancient ideal was finally achieving practicable existence. The case of the Spanish and French colonies was different, but the British colonies in North America had for the most part been left to their own devices.

This may have been due to the unique situation of Great Britain at a critical time in the formation of the colonial culture. The English Civil War, the Great Rebellion, the "Glorious Revolution," the advent of a foreign dynasty (the Hanoverians), and so on, all tended to distract the government in London from the situation "across the pond."

For our purposes we do not have to examine in any depth the reasons why the American colonies developed the way they did — although it is interesting to note that, because king and parliament seemed to spend so much time trying to bring Ireland to heel, they had little time to spare for the American colonies. We only need to appreciate the fact that America represented something new on the world scene, socially, economically — and politically; the vision of "the City on the Hill," in which man could conform himself most closely to his true nature.

Socially, despite the fact that a nobility was grafted on to the social structure, the British colonies of North America probably came closer to a classless society that had grown naturally (as opposed to being imposed artificially by force) than anything that had developed previously in history. This was probably due to the fact that most of the people in the colonies were originally from the middle class. The very poor and the very rich tended not to emigrate. The majority of colonists were drawn from people who wished to obtain ownership of land or other capital, or to better themselves in some other way.

Economically, while there were a significant number of individuals in the southern colonies who were regarded as aristocrats with vast holdings of land, the fact remained that colonial estates were by no means the equal of anything of commensurate size in England, nor were their owners considered all that different from their neighbors. Further, the tone of society was set not by the relatively few wealthy landowners, but by the much larger number of subsistence farmers and small artisans. The largest landowner lived in a fashion little different from his neighboring small proprietor. A subservient class of free tenant farmers was virtually non-existent.

In addition, the large landowners were in a condition that later generations would describe as "land poor." That is, virtually all of their productive wealth was in land, and was difficult to turn into cash, even by mortgage or outright sale. The British colonies, unlike those of Spanish America, had virtually no official circulating media. Most of what existed in the form of coinage found its way into New England in the form of Spanish colonial "Pieces of Eight" — dollars. These usually came into the colonies as "boot" from the "Triangle Trade": molasses, to rum, to slaves. Had it not been for slavery, the third side of the Triangle, Colonial British America would have been one of the most egalitarian societies in history. Aside from that, bills of exchange made up the bulk of the money supply.[1]

The Real Difference

It was, however, in politics that the situation in the colonies of British America differed most significantly from conditions that prevailed in Europe. Having been on their own during their formative period, the colonies had a tradition of self-government. They developed appropriate institutions to support the demands put on the social order by the growth of an egalitarian and largely economically classless society.

As a result, when the British government finally got around to taking a more direct interest in colonial affairs (mainly as a potential source of tax revenue as well as a necessary adjunct for mercantilist policies), the colonists tended to view the increased administrative control as an unwarranted infringement of their rights and liberties as Englishmen. The fact that the common English in England had far fewer effective rights than their American cousins was irrelevant. The colonists were used to being on their own, and doing for themselves. They resented being regarded as a virtual financial milch cow for British commercial and political interests, receiving no perceived benefit in return.

They had been in the habit in many cases of freely assembling and organizing for the common good without interference by or even with the sanction of whatever governing authority existed. Public works were often private

---

[1] Edward S. Kaplan, *The Bank of the United States and the American Economy*. Westport, Connecticut: Greenwood Press, 1999, 1-2.

undertakings, funded and carried out without State assistance. Even the common defense was in many cases much less formal than in Europe, with local militias and the *posse comitatus* taking the place of a standing army or police force.

Now King George III and his parliament viewed these activities not only as infringing on Royal prerogatives, but as an actual danger to the State. Organizing for the common defense was particularly suspicious in light of the Jacobite Rebellion in the 1740s in which "Bonnie Prince Charlie" came very close to regaining the throne for the Stuarts with the support of the Highland clans bearing personal arms. It didn't help any that the British government was in desperate need of money. It had managed to get itself involved in too many European wars at the same time it was trying to expand its colonial empire. As if to maximize the disruption, the nascent Industrial Revolution was starting its generations-long and completely unnecessary social and economic upheaval. Consequently, many traditional practices that the American colonists had long regarded as fundamental rights were limited, abolished, or suspended indefinitely.

Self-Evident Truths

The colonists protested, and (in a story too well known to relate here) went into revolt to protect and maintain those natural rights that they regarded as essential to their dignity as freeborn Englishmen. They had been schooled in these rights by events in the mother country, especially the "Glorious Revolution" at the edge of living memory. The Declaration of Independence was, in fact, closely modeled on the twelve charges by means of which parliament justified taking the throne away from James II Stuart and handing it over to William and Mary. As William Cobbett observed,

> In short, they drew up, *à la* "glorious," charges against their Protestant king, his late Majesty; and as the charges against James II. are found in an Act of Parliament, so the charges against George III. are

found in an Act of Congress, passed on the memorable 4th of July, 1776.[2]

In this, the American Revolution differed significantly from the later French Revolution. This was due in large measure to the completely different understanding of the rights of man and the view of sovereignty.

The American colonists went into revolt to defend themselves against infringement of their natural rights that they had long been in the habit of exercising. The French Revolution (to oversimplify) was, in contrast, the application of new ideas of sovereignty and of the nation State, and the actual institution of a new world order. Despite the repeated statements, possibly even sincere beliefs of America's Founding Fathers, however, the realization of a long-held ideal was not a new world order in the same sense as that represented by the French Revolution.

Thus, the American and French Revolutions differed in at least one important area. The American colonists went into rebellion to protect and defend what they saw as violations on the part of the British Crown of their natural rights as Englishman. In France, the citizens revolted in part in response to the growth of new views of the State and the promulgation of new rights that were not necessarily consistent with the natural moral law, but with "the will of the people."

The American revolutionaries used reason to discern the natural moral law and based their rights on that. The French revolutionaries based their assertion of new rights on "pure reason," without first basing reason itself on a sound foundation. They even went to the unreasonable length of enshrining an actress playing "Reason" as a goddess of the new State-established and maintained religion. The essential difference in orientation is clearly evident when we examine the principles of political science used in forming the United States of America.

---

[2] William Cobbett, *History of the Protestant Reformation in England and Ireland* (1826), § 425.

Natural Law and Rights

When the Virginia Convention met in the spring of 1776, they adopted a resolution to draft a declaration of fundamental natural rights that they believed King George III and his parliament were violating. As George Mason of Gunston Hall in Northern Virginia (near Alexandria) had a reputation as the most experienced legal writer in Virginia, he was the obvious choice to draw up the draft for the discussion and approval of the other delegates. As was his habit, he included a provision that destroyed the legal justification of chattel slavery, even though he was himself a slave owner:

> That all men are by nature equally free and independent, and have certain inherent rights, of which they cannot, by any compact, deprive or divest their posterity; namely, the enjoyment of life and liberty, with the means of acquiring and possessing property, and pursuing and obtaining happiness and safety.

As drafted, the Declaration stated that all men have inherent (*i.e.*, natural) rights, of which neither they nor their posterity can be deprived, regardless of the justification. All men have the right to live, to be free, and to acquire and possess private property: John Locke's famous triad of fundamental human rights of life, liberty, and property — but with a difference.

That difference is the fact that Mason (in common with Bellarmine, whom Mason appears to have studied) simply ignored "state of nature" theory and declared that all men have rights *by nature*, not as a result of entering into a social contract and agreeing to enter into society. Man is political by nature; he does not agree to enter society. He is already a member of society by nature unless he removes himself by the commission of a crime.

George Mason's "Trick"

That man is naturally a member of society is not, however, a doctrine found anywhere in Locke or Sidney. They were firm adherents of the "state of nature" theory, virtually their sole point of agreement with Hobbes. That man is naturally a member of society, however, is found throughout Bellarmine's writings, notably in *De Laicis*.

If *all* men are naturally members of society, regardless of circumstances, it logically follows that this applies to slaves. The clear implication is that slaves — absent conviction of a crime for which the slave is actually and personally guilty — have the natural right to be free. If this sentence in the Virginia declaration passed unchallenged, the implication was that slave owners were themselves engaged in doing the very thing for which they were condemning George III and his parliament.

Even so, Mason might have gotten away with it . . . had he not had the reputation of putting similar insertions into virtually every possible document at every opportunity. By having previously tipped his hand through his laudable habit of standing up to condemn an institution he despised, he made it impossible to slip it in where it would have done the most good. The "reluctant statesman" and even more reluctant slave owner outsmarted himself.

Being familiar with Mason's "tricks," the conservative ("aristocratic") delegates to the Virginia Convention were ready for him. As Robert Rutland described the events surrounding the discussions leading up to the ratification of the Virginia Declaration,

> After each delegate studied the proposals, the general debate opened on a sour note. Thomas Ludwell Lee [Mason's aide on the drafting committee] lamented in his nightly letter-writing sessions that "a certain set of aristocrats" had thrown up a line of defense in an effort to keep control of the Convention in conservative hands. Led by Robert Carter Nicholas, the old guard "kept us at bay on the first line" of the draft, Lee reported. Nicholas challenged the statement that all men are created equally free and independent. In a slaveholding society, the argument ran, all men were obviously not born free and equal. To pretend other-

wise, the conservatives suggested, was to invite civil
war on their own estates.[3]

Consistent with liberal political philosophy, the conservative members amended Mason's language. Raising
the issue of slavery in the very first line of their Declaration could derail the entire Convention. As Florette Henri
reported,

> Those opening words of Mason tore the convention
> apart.
>
> " 'All men are born equally free and independent' —
> pray, what does that mean?" demanded the conserva-
> tive Robert Carter Nicholas. "Does it include my
> slaves?"
>
> Nicholas' supporters joined the outcry. Were slaves to
> be set free? They would not accept such a declaration.
> With one hand it guaranteed Virginians the right to
> hold property, and with the other it snatched that
> property away — slave property. What sort of radical
> document was this? Was it intended to abolish slav-
> ery?
>
> Of course, Mason secretly hoped it might.[4]

Mason was forced to let it pass, or face the very real
possibility that he might undermine the legal justification
of the revolution. As Rutland related,

> As finally approved, the first sentence read "That all
> men are by nature equally free and independent, and
> have certain inherent rights, of which, *when they en-
> ter into a state of society*, they cannot, by any compact,
> deprive or divest their posterity; . . ." The italicized

---

[3] Robert A. Rutland, *George Mason: Reluctant Statesman*. Baton
Rouge, Louisiana: Louisiana State University Press, 1961, 51-
53.

[4] Florette Henri, *George Mason of Virginia*. New York: Crowell-
Collier Press, 1971, 93.

phrase, with its implicit proposition that slaves are not members of society, placated the opposition.[5]

And Property?

While important, however, the focus on slavery and the natural right to be free overshadowed another natural right, "the means of acquiring and possessing property." Unfortunately, property was inextricably tied in with the slavery issue. The institution of black chattel slavery in the United States consisted of owning human beings as private property. To assert a natural right to be free for all men, and then equivocate by keeping some in bondage without the justification that they were convicted criminals was a question not too many people had either the inclination or the ability to deal with. The issue at hand was political freedom for the American colonists, not natural freedom for people unjustly held in slavery.

When you added in the fact that a slave owner believed that his or her economic survival was tied to slavery just as much as to his or her ownership of large tracts of land, discussing slavery and private property at the same time made for an extremely volatile mix. If you asserted that private property in human beings — slavery — is illegitimate, it was a short leap to maintaining that all private property in anything is equally illegitimate.

The important issue here, however, is that Mason laid the groundwork for reconciling the collectivist and individualist positions. He somehow managed to insert the fact that the human person is both individual and social — political — into the Virginia Declaration of Rights. Even though it did not survive unedited, the fact that the idea was there is important — and that it made its way into the underlying political philosophy of the new country via Mason's influence, through Jefferson, on the Declaration of Independence. In the next chapter we will examine how Mason tied private property, slavery, and man as a political animal together into a consistent whole.

---

[5] Rutland, *op. cit.*, 54.

9. Slavery

In the previous chapter we saw that George Mason of Gunston Hall had somehow managed to weave together a consistent political philosophy from a number of seemingly disparate elements. These elements included the individualism of Locke and Sidney, the ultimate (and unconscious) collectivism of Bellarmine — ameliorated and checked by his adherence to the natural moral law based on the Intellect — and, especially, private property and the idea of man as a "political animal."

Mason's synthesis resulted from an understanding of the natural law based on the Intellect — reason. Paradoxically, this was at a time when virtually all intellectuals were following Occam and Grotius and doing the very unintellectual thing of basing the natural law on the Will. Only by basing the law on the Intellect, however (*lex ratio* — "law is reason"), can the natural dignity and sovereignty of the individual be protected, and natural rights remain sacrosanct.

Property v. Slavery

Because it relates to economic life, the most immediate if not the most important aspect of daily life, the natural right to private property was an important factor in Mason's political thought — especially that property he regarded as illegitimate: chattel slavery. Mason had to proceed carefully, however. Calling an ancient institution like chattel slavery into question could very easily undermine the institution of private property itself, to say nothing of making him appear to be a hypocrite — as, in fact, his opponents were quick to claim.

Thomas Jefferson, an estimable, even great individual in many respects, was evidently unable or unwilling to deal with such a thorny issue. Jefferson avoided the issue of property in the Declaration of Independence, and allowed himself to be persuaded to drop a provision abolishing slavery. Otherwise, Jefferson closely followed Mason's lead with respect to the natural moral law.

The dangers associated with attacking chattel slavery (and, in our day, "wage slavery") and thereby undermining recognition of and respect for private property are not as farfetched as they might seem. We can see this in the case of Nathan C. Kouns.

Kouns, a devout Catholic, supported slavery and served as a Major in the Confederate Army during the American Civil War. He was evidently able to accept the equivocations of the southern American bishops in their anxiety to assure their flocks that the condemnation of chattel slavery by Pope Gregory XVI in the 1839 Constitution *In Supremo* ("Constitution" being a teaching, not a political, document in this context) did not apply to slavery as practiced in the United States.

The southern American Catholic bishops assuaged their consciences and those of the faithful with the equivocation that the Papal Constitution only condemned the international slave *trade*, not slavery itself — as if employing slaves as labor, and dealing in them as a commodity were somehow morally different! Of course, an objective reading of the Constitution would have corrected this obvious error, as would reference to the numerous papal condemnations of slavery prior to that date.[1]

After the Civil War, Kouns seems to have become convinced that, because private property in human beings is wrong, *all* private property is wrong. Kouns then promoted socialism — the abolition of private property — as consistent with Catholic doctrine. He wrote two historical novels to present his case, *Arius the Libyan, An Idyl [sic] of the Primitive Church* (1883), and *Dorcas, the Daughter of Faustina* (1884), both of which enjoyed reasonably good sales into the 1920s.

---

[1] *Vide* Rev. Joel S. Panzer, *The Popes and Slavery*. New York: Alba House, 1996.

The novels are competently written, and (if not exactly great literature) have convinced a number of critics and commentators that, despite their flat contradiction of Catholic doctrine, they detail authentic Catholic teaching regarding private property. It would not be too far-fetched to discover that Pope Leo XIII (who seems to have considered the United States something unique and special) was aware of the novels and the effect they had when he wrote *Rerum Novarum*.[2] The 1891 encyclical is built around a series of explicit statements reaffirming private property as a natural right, the same as life, liberty, and "pursuit of happiness" (the acquisition and development of virtue).

Fundamental Rights

As the draft of the Virginia Declaration of Rights clearly demonstrates, however, Mason attempted to insert into the resolution a respect for the human dignity of every individual, not just a select majority or minority. It is thus probably due more to Mason than to Jefferson that the American Republic is based on the Thomist, rather than the Occamist concept of the natural law (that is, Intellect or Nature over Will or Revelation). Mason was instrumental in making certain that the new Constitution of 1789 included a bill of fundamental natural rights, although the effort was spearheaded by fellow Virginian James Madison, whom many Constitutional scholars thereby credit with the first ten amendments.

The problem was that Madison doesn't seem to have had an equal understanding with Mason of the need to make certain that the institution of private property has the same protections as every other natural right. This left a serious problem in place, giving an either/or aspect to the slavery issue: either immediate and full emancipation, or nothing. The problem was that disaster would result in either event. As Helen Hill explained the situation in her biography of Mason, describing a conversation between Jefferson and Mason and witnessed by Philip Mazzei,

---

[2] Leo XIII, *Rerum Novarum* ("On Labor and Capital"), 1891.

Philip Mazzei's "Memoirs" give an intimate picture of
the two arguing these contrasting aspects of the problem, taking sides, one suspects, chiefly to clarify the
issues. Jefferson was advocating abolition, arguing
that

It was demanded as much by humanity as by justice;
that to keep in slavery beings born with rights equal
to ours and who did not differ from us in anything but
color, was an injustice not only barbarous and cruel,
but even shameful, especially when they risked everything in helping us gain our freedom.

Mason and Mazzei dissented from this view:

Mr. George Mason said much more; and he showed
the necessity of educating them before taking such a
step, teaching them to make good use of their freedom. "Each one of us knows," he said, "that the ne-
groes considered the work as punishment." He also
convinced us that if they were not educated before being freed, the first use they would make of their liberty would be loafing, and hence they would become
thieves out of necessity.

In the course of the Richmond debates, Mason fought
the Constitution clause by clause, but his most effective oratory was reserved for the slavery provision.[3]

Education and gradual emancipation might not satisfy
the purists on either side, but it was the common sense
approach, and had the potential to respect at least to
some degree both the property of the slaveholders and the
right of the slaves to liberty. Mason was punctilious in
bringing property into the discussion. Owners of slaves
had acquired their property legally and, consistent with
popular belief for thousands of years, legitimately. To
dismiss this by mandating immediate emancipation, even
with compensation offered to the slaveholders, could call

[3] Helen Hill, *George Mason, Constitutionalist*. Cambridge, Massachusetts: Harvard University Press, 1938, 217-218.

property itself into question. By taking the expedient route and omitting all mention of property from the Bill of Rights, Madison undermined a very important natural right.

Mason, however, understood that man is both social and individual — a *political* animal, who only reaches his full potential by associating with other individuals and groups of his kind in the *pólis*, an organized and formally legislated community.

Theory v. Practice

Still, Mason lived in a society that, while it paid lip service to the theory of the equality of all men, rejected that same equality in practice. Many of the Founding Fathers assumed, with Locke and Sidney, that society is not natural to man. The liberal theory is that you accept infringement of certain rights when you agree to enter society in order to protect what remains.

Paradoxically, the idea that man outside society has all rights and accepts infringement in order to gain some measure of protection abolishes the concept of natural rights in the same breath that purports to defend it. An infringement of a right that can presumably be *exercised* absolutely is not the same as a limitation on the exercise of a right that is *possessed* absolutely, that is, inalienably. The former constitutes a tacit admission that possession of the right is not, after all, natural or absolute, while the latter is the normal working of the *politikos bios*, the "life of the citizen in the State." This in part consists of properly defining and limiting (not infringing on) the exercise of absolute rights so that humanity can live together in peace . . . *naturally*.

The liberal position is that anyone who has not been admitted to society cannot be recognized as a person, that is, as having rights. Consequently, most of the Founding Fathers accepted the "state of nature" theory common to Locke and Sidney, and their chief opponent, Hobbes. Mason understood that this made true equality impossible. This is because if you wished to keep someone in an unequal state such as slavery, you merely had to assert that members of a particular group, or even the group itself, had not entered society.

Are Rights Absolute?

Further, asserting a state of nature in which man not only possesses natural rights absolutely, but has the absolute (that is, unlimited) exercise thereof argues that the unlimited exercise of all rights is natural. This we know is impossible. One of the primary "laws" of the common good (that is, of social justice), second only to the demand that the common good itself remain inviolate, is that no right or power can legitimately be exercised in any way that harms the right holder, other individuals or groups, or the common good itself. Limitation of the exercise of rights, even of rights that are possessed absolutely, is thus inherent in human nature itself.

Man's political nature is exhibited by his membership in a single group or (in practical terms) many groups that, in part, make up the common good and demonstrate the organized structure of society. The mere fact of a group itself is sufficient proof that someone is a member of society and is, in the truest sense, political. The moment you make conditions, that is, once you declare that personality is due to something other than mere humanity, you are, essentially, denying that man is political by nature, as well as undermining the natural moral law.

Fortunately, however, Mason had an inherent understanding of the importance of groups. He realized that true political action consists of something more than simply passing and enforcing laws. Mason's remarkable accomplishment was to insert Aristotle's concept of man as a political animal into a supremely individualistic culture and intellectual framework. He was able to find a middle ground and develop a synthesis between liberal philosophy's state of nature, and Cardinal Bellarmine's concept that God grants certain rights to the collective.

Mason's *via media* was not articulated. It is, however, powerfully evident in his draft of the Virginia Declaration of Rights, his insistence on a bill of fundamental natural rights in the U.S. Constitution, and, fortunately, in his influence on the founding document of the United States: the Declaration of Independence.

Mason can therefore be given at least partial credit for the way in which the American approach to government and politics developed immediately following the Revolution. As we will see in the next chapter, in America private property, free association, and the idea of groups were combined in a unique new way that developed a new science of politics. It also gave hints of a new concept in moral philosophy, the idea of "social virtue," that is, legal justice as a particular, not merely a general virtue, with an "act" that can affect the institutions of the common good directly, instead of indirectly by working only on the general "tone" of society.

10. Democracy in America

In 1835, Alexis de Tocqueville published the first volume of what is generally considered the first major work of sociology, *Democracy in America*. The book is a remarkable study that seems to be little appreciated today for its true worth. This was followed in 1840 by the second volume. *Democracy in America* is a work that many authorities agree paints an unparalleled portrait of the United States after the first rush of revolutionary ardor had cooled. De Tocqueville chronicled a time when the country got down to the work of building a new type of nation — one that respects the dignity of the individual as well as the demands of the common good.

While there are de Tocqueville societies in the United States, their stated function is to encourage individual private charity for worthy causes, thereby obviating the presumed necessity for State assistance. This is a distant and foggy understanding of de Tocqueville's analysis of what American democracy meant in the 1830s. Taking de Tocqueville's observations about America as manifestations of individual philanthropy may even serve to blunt our full awareness of de Tocqueville's achievement, as well as our comprehension of how the people of that day understood what it meant to be an American.

We can appreciate de Tocqueville's analysis properly only by referencing George Mason's tacit reconciliation, in the Virginia Declaration of Rights and the U.S. Constitution, of humanity as both individual and social — that is, political — in nature. De Tocqueville took as his thesis that in America western civilization saw something entirely new on the stage of history, something that transcended the usual conflict between individualism and collectivism. In England, for example, government and great works were considered the bailiwick of individuals, while

in France people looked to the State for virtually everything.

New Things

The distinctive manner in which Americans related to
their institutions and to the common good as a whole is
the subject matter of *Democracy in America*. This they did
not purely as individuals, nor as mere cogs in the machinery of the State, but in a way uniquely human: *politically*.
Nor was this in the incomplete sense that Aristotle assumed, a limited and indirect access to the common good.
Americans somehow had what appeared to be full and
direct access to the common good.

Society was thus not the chaotic mess that many European commentators affected to observe in the United
States. On the contrary, democracy in America appeared
to operate by definite rules in conformity with the natural
moral law, many of which de Tocqueville described. As he
explained,

> It may fairly be believed that a certain number of
> Americans pursue a peculiar form of worship from
> habit more than from conviction. In the United States
> the sovereign authority is religious, and consequently
> hypocrisy must be common; but there is no country in
> the world where the Christian religion retains a
> greater influence over the souls of men than in Ameri-
> ca; and there can be no greater proof of its utility and
> of its conformity to human nature than that its influ-
> ence is powerfully felt over the most enlightened and
> free nation of the earth.[1]

De Tocqueville discerned a number of "rules" by means
of which democracy is maintained in America — or at
least was maintained in the America of the 1830s. Many
of these are intimately connected with the necessity of
restoring the natural law and maintaining freedom of association. De Tocqueville observed freedom of association

---

[1] "Causes Which Tend to Maintain Democracy," Volume I, Ch.
XVII.

as the chief characteristic of American life. He saw it consistent with liberty, although inspired by the drive for equality. This, according to de Tocqueville, was a situation that, while in many respects superficially similar to what prevailed in Europe, was actually something new on the world scene, and something vital to the survival of democracy. As he declared,

> The first of the duties that are at this time imposed upon those who direct our affairs is to educate democracy, to reawaken, if possible, its religious beliefs; to purify its morals; to mold its actions; to substitute a knowledge of statecraft for its inexperience, and an awareness of its true interest for its blind instincts, to adapt its government to time and place, and to modify it according to men and to conditions. A new science of politics is needed for a new world.[2]

The Laws of Democracy

First, an orderly society is of the utmost importance. That network of institutions within which each individual carries out even the most mundane aspects of life, thereby working to acquire and develop virtue, must be maintained. This is consistent with Aquinas's observation in *De Regimine Principum* that social order is a great good — so great, in fact, that we must be willing to submit to great injustice, even tyranny, if removal of the tyranny or correction of the injustice will cause material harm to the social order. This is because the business of daily life, of acquiring and developing virtue (whether at the lowest level of subsistence, or the highest of self-actualization), requires an orderly society. As de Tocqueville explained,

> The passions that agitate the Americans most deeply are not their political, but their commercial passions; or, rather, they introduce the habits of business into their political life. They love order, without which affairs do not prosper; and they set an especial value

---

[2] "Author's Introduction," Volume I.

upon regular conduct, which is the foundation of a solid business.[3]

Second, despite their oft-touted individualism, Americans had a strong tendency to subsume their private interests, join with others, and cooperate in order to achieve a desired end. As de Tocqueville explained,

> When the members of a community are forced to attend to public affairs, they are necessarily drawn from the circle of their own interests and snatched at times from self-observation. As soon as a man begins to treat of public affairs in public, he begins to perceive that he is not so independent of his fellow men as he had at first imagined, and that in order to obtain their support he must often lend them his co-operation.[4]

Third, Americans had integrated into their social habits the principle that, in order to optimize one's particular good, they first had to secure the common good. That is, Americans had somehow concluded that each individual's primary particular good consisted of his or her place in the common good, and that the general welfare is, in a real sense, each person's particular welfare. This is because the complex network of institutions that make up the common good are the chief means by which each individual acquires and develops virtue, and so benefits him- or herself. As de Tocqueville explained,

> A man comprehends the influence which the well-being of his country has upon his own; he is aware that the laws permit him to contribute to that prosperity, and he labors to promote it, first because it benefits him, and secondly because it is in part his own work.[5]

---

[3] "Causes Which Tend to Maintain Democracy," Volume I, Ch. XVII.

[4] "That the Americans Combat the Effects of Individualism by Free Institutions," Volume II, Book II, Ch. IV.

[5] "Advantages of Democracy: Public Spirit in the United States," Volume I, Ch. XIV.

Fourth, de Tocqueville noted that every American as a general rule believed him- or herself to be personally responsible for the condition of society. If something needed fixing, it was the individual's responsibility to do something, not sit around waiting for somebody else to undertake the task. In consequence, when a situation came up that required correction, individuals either handled it alone, or organized with their neighbors and got on with the job. As de Tocqueville described this tendency,

> The citizen of the United States is taught from infancy to rely upon his own exertions in order to resist the evils and the difficulties of life; he looks upon the social authority with an eye of mistrust and anxiety, and he claims its assistance only when he is unable to do without it. This habit may be traced even in the schools, where the children in their games are wont to submit to rules which they have themselves established, and to punish misdemeanors which they have themselves defined. The same spirit pervades every act of social life. If a stoppage occurs in a thoroughfare and the circulation of vehicles is hindered, the neighbors immediately form themselves into a deliberative body; and this extemporaneous assembly gives rise to an executive power which remedies the inconvenience before anybody has thought of recurring to a pre-existing authority superior to that of the persons immediately concerned.[6]

Fifth, Americans had internalized what today is known as the "principle of subsidiarity." That is, they realized that the agency to handle social situations is not automatically the highest or the lowest level of society, but the one closest to the situation. Thus, the "higher" institutions, such as the state or the federal governments, should never take over the functions properly assigned to local institutions. Further (something de Tocqueville was to highlight later in *The Old Régime and the French Revolution*,

---

[6] "Political Associations in the United States," Volume I, Ch. XII.

1856), neither should "lower" institutions take over the function of the "higher" ones. As de Tocqueville explained,

> The township, taken as a whole, and in relation to the central government, in only an individual, like any other to whom the theory [sovereignty of the people] I have just described is applicable. Municipal independence in the United States is therefore a natural consequence of the very principle of the sovereignty of the people. All the American republics [de Tocqueville characterizes the individual states as "republics"] recognize it more or less, but circumstances have peculiarly favored its growth in New England.
>
> In this part of the Union political life had its origin in the townships; and it may almost be said that each of them originally formed an independent nation. When the kings of England afterwards asserted their supremacy, they were content to assume the central power of the State. They left the townships where they were before; and although they are now subject to the State, they were not at first, or were hardly so. They did not receive their powers from the central authority, but, on the contrary, they gave up a portion of their independence to the State. This is an important distinction and one that the reader must constantly recollect. The townships are generally subordinate to the State only in those interests which I shall term *social*, as they are common to all the others. They are independent in all that concerns themselves alone; and among the inhabitants of New England I believe that not a man is to be found who would acknowledge that the State has any right to interfere in their town affairs.[7]

Free Association

Sixth, possibly the most striking characteristic of American life as far as de Tocqueville was concerned was the

---

[7] "Townships and Municipal Bodies," Volume I, Ch. V.

incredible proclivity to organize and form associations. As he observed,

> In no country in the world has the principle of association been more successfully used or applied to a greater multitude of objects than in America. Besides the permanent associations which are established by law under the names of townships, cities, and counties, a vast number of others are formed and maintained by the agency of private individuals.[8]

Seventh, and finally (at least for our limited purposes), this habit of forming associations was so great that Americans of the 1830s, according to de Tocqueville, couldn't even imagine doing things differently. If something needed to be done, and it was at all important, it was vital that people organize and form themselves into associations in order to accomplish whatever end they had in mind. Thus, as de Tocqueville explained,

> The political associations that exist in the United States are only a single feature in the midst of the immense assemblage of associations in that country. Americans of all ages, all conditions, and all dispositions constantly form associations. They have not only commercial and manufacturing companies, in which all take part, but associations of a thousand other kinds, religious, moral, serious, futile, general or restricted, enormous or diminutive. The Americans make associations to give entertainments, to found seminaries, to build inns, to construct churches, to diffuse books, to send missionaries to the antipodes; in this manner they found hospitals, prisons, and schools. If it is proposed to inculcate some truth or to foster some feeling by the encouragement of a great example, they form a society. Wherever at the head of some new undertaking you see the government in France, or a man of rank in England, in the United States you will be sure to find an association. . . . The

---

[8] "Political Associations in the United States," Volume I, Ch. XII.

English often perform great things singly, whereas the Americans form associations for the smallest undertakings. It is evident that the former people consider association as a powerful means of action, but the latter seem to regard it as the only means they have of acting.[9]

It should therefore come as no surprise that the intellectual elite of Europe (at least those most closely in touch with the Thomist and Aristotelian concept of the natural moral law, such as Pope Leo XIII), saw in the United States a great sign of hope, even (as Abraham Lincoln was to characterize it in the next generation in his Second Inaugural Address), the last, best hope of mankind. We will begin to look at how the United States both lived up to that expectation and fell short of it in the next chapter.

---

[9] "Of the Use Which the Americans Make of Public Associations in Civil Life," Volume II, Book II, Ch. V.

11. City on a Hill

In the previous chapter we discovered that a society had developed in the United States of the 1830s that appeared to adhere more closely to the natural moral law based on the divine Intellect (Nature) than at any previous time or under any other arrangement in history. As Alexis de Tocqueville analyzed the situation, "By the side of every religion is to be found a political opinion, which is connected with it by affinity. If the human mind be left to follow its own bent, it will regulate the temporal and spiritual institutions of society in a uniform manner, and man will endeavor, if I may so speak, to *harmonize* earth with heaven."[1]

The Basis of Society

Surprisingly, perhaps even shockingly to today's liberal who detects a lurking and insidious evil in public displays or expressions of religion of any sect, but who singles out the Catholic Church as especially obnoxious in this regard, de Tocqueville professed to see in Catholicism a particular affinity for and support of the best in American democracy. According to de Tocqueville, the Catholic population of the United States, particularly those of Irish birth or descent, while a minority, provided the country with a solid core of citizens who were, at one and the same time, both independent minded, and submissive to good laws that promoted equality and social order. De Tocqueville claimed that in America, even where strict observance of Catholic practices according to the letter of the law faded or was non-existent (as among Protestants and adherents of other faiths), nowhere was there strong-

---

[1] "Causes Which Tend to Maintain Democracy: Religion Considered as a Political Institution Which Powerfully Contributes to the Maintenance of a Democratic Republic Among the Americans," Volume I, Ch. XVII.

er adherence to the *spirit* of Catholicism, even among non-Catholics, particularly when conforming political institutions to the precepts of the natural moral law.[2]

Nor was de Tocqueville alone in his opinion that Americans had somehow reconciled humanity's social and individual natures. Immediately following the Civil War, Orestes Brownson published his own study of the United States, *The American Republic* (1865). Brownson, with Emerson and Thoreau considered one of the "top three" Transcendentalists in the United States until he converted to Catholicism in the 1840s and was swept under the rug of history, was even more explicit than de Tocqueville in his belief that America represented something genuinely new.

Once the country corrected (more or less) its "original sin" of chattel slavery with the bloodiest war in American history, the stage was set for America to fulfill its true purpose. Brownson believed that the United States was chosen by God to continue reconciling humanity's individual and social natures and provide, as far as humanly possible, the ideal environment within which man could become more fully himself. As Brownson put it in the introduction to the book that he considered his finest achievement,

> The United States, or the American Republic, has a mission, and is chosen of God for the realization of a great idea. It has been chosen not only to continue the work assigned to Greece and Rome, but to accomplish a greater work than was assigned to either. In art, it will prove false to its mission if it do not rival Greece; and in science and philosophy, if it do not surpass it. In the State, in law, in jurisprudence, it must continue and surpass Rome. Its idea is liberty, indeed, but liberty with law, and law with liberty. Yet its mission is not so much the realization of liberty as the realization of the true idea of the State, which secures at once the authority of the public and the freedom of the

[2] *Ibid.*

individual — the sovereignty of the people without social despotism, and individual freedom without anarchy. In other words, its mission is to bring out in its
life the dialectic union of authority and liberty, of the
natural rights of man and those of society. The Greek
and Roman republics asserted the State to the detriment of individual freedom; modern republics either
do the same, or assert individual freedom to the detriment of the State. The American republic has been
instituted by Providence to realize the freedom of each
with advantage to the other.[3]

Despite some vagueness in terminology regarding social
rights, *Democracy in America* and *The American Republic*
share common assumptions. Chief among these is that
the human person and thus the State, a human artifact,
are based on and must conform to God's Nature, even
when not following someone's interpretation of what may
(or may not) be God's Will. Where de Tocqueville focused
on the sociological aspects of a government of the people,
by the people, and for the people, however, Brownson ex-
plored political philosophy and science.

Complements

De Tocqueville and Brownson are not in competition.
Both *Democracy in America* and *The American Republic*
should be read as necessary complements to each other.
De Tocqueville, for example, appeared to assume as a giv-
en that when he referred to "Catholic political philosophy"
his predominantly French and presumably Catholic read-
ers knew what he was talking about. On the other hand,
Brownson, addressing an audience composed largely of
non-Catholics, went to great lengths to explain of what
that philosophy consists and why the American Republic
embodied Catholic political philosophy to a greater degree
than any previous State in history.

------

[3] Orestes Brownson, "Introduction," *The American Republic*,
1865.

Similarly, Brownson's audience in 1865 consisted primarily of small landowners and other proprietors who were fully aware of the importance of private property as the chief support for other natural rights, such as life, liberty, and pursuit of happiness (*i.e.*, the acquisition and development of virtue). Other than to explain some technicalities about property and its importance as a natural right and to condemn both socialism and capitalism, Brownson spent very little space on ownership and private property. Nevertheless, he clearly considered widespread direct ownership of the means of production critical to the survival of a healthy State and a moral social order — hence his devastating critique of what he considered the deadly poison of socialism:

> It wears a pious aspect, it has divine words on its lips, and almost unction in its speech. It is not easy for the unlearned to detect its fallacy, and the great body of the people are prepared to receive it as Christian truth. We cannot deny it without seeming to them to be warring against the true interests of society, and also against the Gospel of our Lord. Never was heresy more subtle, more adroit, better fitted for success. How skillfully it flatters the people! It is said, the saints shall judge the world. By the change of a word, the people are transformed into saints, and invested with the saintly character and office. How adroitly, too, it appeals to the people's envy and hatred of their superiors, and to their love of the world, without shocking their orthodoxy or wounding their piety! Surely Satan has here, in Socialism, done his best, almost outdone himself, and would, if it were possible, deceive the very elect, so that no flesh should be saved.[4]

Brownson, of course, did not have to deal with today's modernists and positivists and their word games, or the circumlocutions employed by both capitalists and social-

---

[4] *Essays and Reviews Chiefly on Theology, Politics, and Socialism,* 1852.

ists to try and whitewash their dogmatic beliefs under different names, such as "democratic capitalism (or socialism)," "solidarism," or even "Christian socialism." No, Brownson knew exactly what socialism is, and defined it the same way as Karl Marx in *The Communist Manifesto*: the abolition of private property in the means of production. In the America of Brownson's day, no person considered sane questioned the importance of private property in the means of production, whether or not he or she agreed that direct ownership of capital should be widespread.

De Tocqueville, on the other hand, wrote primarily for a French and English audience, both countries in which the tradition of small ownership had been eroded for centuries, as William Cobbett frequently pointed out in his polemical works. Consequently, de Tocqueville stressed far more than Brownson the importance of widespread direct ownership of the means of production as the chief support for other natural rights.

From Agricultural to Industry

The problem, of course, is obvious, at least in hindsight. The Industrial Revolution had received a great impetus in the United States due to the Civil War. Many authorities, then as now, credited the Union victory to the industrial and commercial might of the North. In mid-century, however, relatively few people were directly engaged in industrial and commercial enterprises, even as wage earners. Contrary to the assertions of David Christy in *Cotton is King* (1855), even in the South before the war, relatively few people — including slaves — were employed on plantations engaged in the production of goods, services, and commodities for the international market. Most slaveholders owned less than a dozen slaves, usually only one or two, and were engaged in subsistence agriculture or production of goods and services for the local market. The vast majority of the population, North and South, were engaged in subsistence agriculture, artisan type production of goods, or kept small shops.

All of this changed with Abraham Lincoln's 1862 Homestead Act and the opening of the "Great American Desert" to settlement — and as a vast new market for the goods being produced in the increasingly industrialized East. The Homestead Act changed the essential character of American agriculture from subsistence farming supplemented with small "cash crops," to production primarily for market, with basic necessities purchased instead of being homegrown.

Laura Ingalls Wilder brilliantly chronicled this change in her "Little House" books. The assumption is now so engrained in American tax and agricultural policy that in 1948, the decision in the landmark case *Wickard v. Filburn*,[5] that greatly increased the economic power of the federal government, held that all agricultural production, even that which was consumed on the farm where it was produced, was subject to the interstate commerce clause, whether or not it was produced for market. Similarly, as the settlement of the West opened up new markets, the pace of industrialization increased. Settlement and industrialization not only complemented each other, neither would have been possible — or, at least, as successful — without the other.

Misunderstanding Money

Unfortunately, while agricultural capital — land — was broadly owned, with the ownership base rapidly expanding due to the Homestead Act, ownership of the new and growing commercial and industrial enterprises was becoming increasingly concentrated. By 1905, when Judge Peter Stenger Grosscup, one of Theodore Roosevelt's "Trust Busters," wrote a series of articles addressing the situation, small ownership of commerce and industry had, for all practical purposes, disappeared as a feature of American life.[6]

---

[5] 317 U.S. 111 (1942).
[6] *Vide* Peter S. Grosscup, "How to Save the Corporation," *McClure's Magazine*, February, 1905, reprinted in *Curing World*

Concentration of ownership of what was becoming responsible for the bulk of production of marketable goods, services, and commodities built a serious conflict into the system. As Louis Kelso and Mortimer Adler pointed out three-quarters of a century later in *The Capitalist Manifesto*[7] and *The New Capitalists*,[8] concentrated ownership is not due to some law of nature, as both capitalists and socialists assume even to this day. On the contrary, concentrated ownership of the means of production is directly attributable to a fundamental misunderstanding of money and credit, and thus a misapplication of incorrect assumptions to the task of financing capital formation, whether that capital is in the form of industrial, commercial, or agricultural assets.

Rule of Law

This misunderstanding about money and credit has a profound influence on how people view the political process. Nowhere is this more evident than in the work of two Englishmen, Walter Bagehot and Albert Venn Dicey. Briefly (for this is not the place to get into an in-depth analysis of the differences between the two), Bagehot, who expressed great disdain for the United States, was a firm adherent of State-controlled monopoly capitalism (described in his book, *Lombard Street*, 1873) — with the State itself controlled by "the money interests." Clearly taking the "law is will" position (*lex voluntas*), Bagehot advocated a form of "democracy" in which, consistent with the principles laid out by Thomas Hobbes in *Leviathan*, the commercial and financial elite rather than the hereditary monarchy or aristocracy controlled the country, as was the case in India before the Great Mutiny.[9] Not surprisingly, Bagehot was an adherent of the British Currency School, a "proto-Chartalist." He defined "money" essen-

---

Poverty: The New Role of Property, Rev. John H. Miller, ed., St. Louis, Missouri: Social Justice Review, 1994, 35-44.

[7] New York: Random House, 1958.

[8] New York: Random House, 1961,

[9] Walter Bagehot, *The English Constitution*. Sussex, UK: Sussex Academic Press, 1997.

tially as a State-authorized purchase order, an exercise of
property by the State in the private wealth of the country,
not as an offer and acceptance as a true contract.

Dicey, Bagehot's most effective philosophical opponent,
was a firm believer in the rule of law, and popularized the
term on both sides of the Atlantic. A great admirer of the
United States, Dicey paid an extended visit to the U.S. in
the 1870s. Bagehot never visited America. Dicey, however, unfortunately avoided the economic issue. He focused
on purely political matters. This may have been as a result of the inevitable conflict between a democratic political system, and an absolutist economic system.

For whatever reason, Dicey, a firm adherent of the law
is reason position (*lex ratio*), did not address the problems
inherent in applying the elitist and undemocratic principles of the Currency School to a presumably democratic
political system. Dicey's classic, *An Introduction to the
Study of the Law of the Constitution* (1886), simply avoids
the whole issue of economics, although he was appointed
one of the first professors at the new London School of
Economics in 1896. Dicey's *Conflict of Laws*, published
that same year, concentrates largely on what is today
known as "business law." It does not discuss the conflict
between the two schools of monetary thought. On the other hand, *Lectures on the Relation Between Law and Public
Opinion in England During the Nineteenth Century* (1905)
is a brilliant analysis of the principle of subsidiarity, and
its relation to the sovereignty of the individual manifested
through membership in groups.

Banking in America

Incorrect assumptions about money, credit, and finance
were built into the American system following the Civil
War. Part of this was due to Treasury Secretary Salmon
Chase's controversial decision to finance the Union war
effort primarily through borrowing instead of taxation.[10]

---

[10] Charles A. Conant, *A History of Modern Banks of Issue.* New
York: G. P. Putnam's Sons, 1927, 403.

There was, however, also the problem of the chaotic banking system, a situation made infinitely worse by the President Andrew Jackson's pyrrhic victory in his war against the Second Bank of the United States in the previous generation.

The National Bank Act of 1864, modeled on the British Bank Charter Act of 1844, did bring a measure of order to the financial system. Unfortunately the National Bank Act, in common with Sir Robert Peel's Bank Charter Act, embodied two false assumptions about money, credit and finance that were to have serious repercussions in the decades to come, culminating in the "Panic of 1907."

These were, one, that "money," contrary to the natural moral law based on the Intellect, is — and can only be — a purchase order issued by the State or a State-authorized individual or entity. Two, that capital formation can only be financed out of existing accumulations of savings. With this in mind, the subtitle of Kelso and Adler's above-referenced second book, *The New Capitalists*, is revealing: "A Proposal to Free Economic Growth from the Slavery of Savings."

These two assumptions, widely accepted even today, flatly contradict the true nature of money as the medium of exchange linked through private property to the present value of existing and future marketable goods and services, and the science of finance as based on a regulated system of secured promises, with or without existing accumulations of savings. The new elitist assumptions about money and credit — the life's blood of the community — came into direct conflict with the democratic American political system, with results that became ever more destructive of political and social stability as the century wore on.

Unfortunately, as the damage increased, people began to forget or ignore the basic principles and "rules" of democracy in America as discerned by de Tocqueville, and the true origin and transmission of the sovereign power as described by Brownson. In view of the apparent helplessness of the individual seemingly trapped in an impersonal system, people began to look to the State as the agency that alone could ameliorate the increasing disorder in society.

12. Birth of a Nation

As we saw in the previous chapter, following the Civil War the social order in the United States was more closely attuned to the natural moral law, and the country was better positioned to take advantage of this orientation than any previous nation or people in history. The essential elements of an economically (and thus politically) just society were, to all appearances, firmly in place.

Unlimited Role of the State

There were some serious flaws, of course. The federal government was taking a more active role in the economy. This was due primarily to the increased power it had gained as a result of the war. Agitation on the part of organized labor increased. This was a necessary counter to the growing power of concentrated ownership of the means of production in industrial and commercial assets in the hands of a relatively small class of capitalists. Unfortunately, organized labor concentrated not on gaining power through ownership for the working classes, but on using the coercive power of the State to enforce better conditions and higher wages. The property rights of small owners were being rapidly eroded as the State and the new capitalist class joined forces to rebuild the economy and stabilize the currency after the war.

Perhaps most important, the widespread direct ownership achieved by means of the Homestead Act was not able to provide ownership opportunities for everyone, nor did it apply to anything other than land. Three factors were responsible for this. One, the amount of land available for homesteading was limited. Two, not everyone is cut out to be a farmer. Three, an increasing proportion of the production of marketable goods and services was coming not from agriculture (although agricultural production was phenomenal), but out of industry and commerce. The proportion of people making a living as farmers was decreasing even as farm ownership was rapidly expanding.

Thus, even though the Homestead Act was one of the greatest economic achievements in history, it came at a time when its effect was diluted by its lack of universal applicability. Ironically, the benefits of the Homestead Act would be almost completed negated in less than fifty years by the incredible expansion of industry and commerce in the United States — an expansion in which, unlike that of the agricultural sector, the great mass of people did not have any opportunity to participate.

Statism and Socialism

Consequently, the doctrines of socialism swiftly began gaining ground, even in the United States. This was all the more insidious in that many adherents of what was and remains effectively socialism were honestly and sincerely convinced that what they advocated was not socialism at all, but a new, if extremely vague thing they called "social justice."

A great deal of this confusion was caused by the virtually complete abandonment of the natural moral law based on Nature (Intellect or Reason) as the basis for the social order. Taking its place was either a weak and ineffectual natural law based on the Will, or one of the many theories of government that sought to remove God completely from the equation.

A great deal of the blame for the rapid growth of socialism, even when the socialism was not recognized as such, can be placed on the almost universal misunderstanding of the institutions of private property, and thus money, credit, and finance. Of all the misconceptions about these fundamentally simple concepts, however, two were more destructive than all the others.

As we have already noted, these were (and remain) one, the idea that "money" is a purchase order issued by the State or a State-authorized individual or entity, and two, that existing accumulations of savings are necessary to finance capital formation. The first abolishes private property, while the second raises an almost insurmountable barrier against ownership of the means of production by people who are not already wealthy.

First, we have already demonstrated that the definition of "money" used by the British Currency School, and which led to the insanity of Chartalism,[1] gives the State effective ownership of everything. The second, while asserted as dogmatically as the definition of money, is equally false — even though, in common with the tenets of the British Currency School, it is a cornerstone of Keynesian, as well as Monetarist and Austrian economics, and virtually everything in between.

The Slavery of Savings

This is because the assumption that only existing accumulations of savings can be used to finance capital formation necessarily results in the dogmatic assertion that wealth must therefore be concentrated in as few hands as possible. This is either in a private elite of capitalists, or in the hands of a presumably beneficent State or State-substitute. As Keynes asserted without any proof in *The Economic Consequences of the Peace* (1919), the book that established his reputation,

> The immense accumulations of fixed capital which, to the great benefit of mankind, were built up during the half century before the war, could never have come about in a Society where wealth was divided equitably.[2]

The reasoning behind this assertion is logical — once we accept the incorrect belief that only existing accumulations of savings can be used to finance capital formation. Savings in this paradigm is, as Dr. Harold Moulton pointed out in *The Formation of Capital*,[3] *always* defined as cutting consumption — *always*. This means that, in order

---

[1] *Vide* Georg Friedrich Knapp, *The State Theory of Money*. London: Macmillan & Company, Ltd., 1924.
[2] *The Economic Consequences of the Peace*, 2.III.
[3] Washington, DC: The Brookings Institution, 1935, 37-41.

to have sufficient savings to form new capital, we need a class of people who cannot consume all they produce, and who are forced to reinvest the excess in additional capital, thereby accelerating their accumulation of unconsumed and unconsumable wealth. As technology becomes increasingly complex and expensive relative to the earning power of the average citizen, ownership of the means of production becomes increasingly concentrated first in the hands of the rich, then the super rich, then the ultra rich.

Thus, as the 19th century entered its final quarter, increasing numbers of people, even in the United States, reacted to the obvious abuses of capitalism. More and more people began looking to the State not only as the secondary or backup guardian of a well-ordered common good, but as the primary provider and guarantor of all individual goods and personal wellbeing. This was a far cry from the attitudes and habits of Americans described by de Tocqueville and Brownson, and all in the space of less than a quarter century.

The Last, Best Hope

Nevertheless, the United States was, for all its faults, still seen by many people as the best hope of mankind. Nowhere was this more evident — or, to many people, more surprising — than in the writings of the popes, the heads of the Catholic Church, beginning with the pontificate of Leo XIII, whose work we will examine as coming from a moral authority, with no reference to his religious role.

In his first "encyclical," Pope Leo XIII blamed the terrible social and economic conditions on the virtual complete abandonment of the natural moral law as the guiding principle of government. Encyclicals are certain teaching documents issued by the popes. As he explained in *Inscrutabili* ("On the Evils Afflicting Modern Society"), issued a short time after his election in 1878,

> Now, the source of these evils lies chiefly, We are convinced, in this, that the holy and venerable authority of the Church, which in God's name rules mankind,

upholding and defending all lawful authority, has been despised and set aside. The enemies of public order, being fully aware of this, have thought nothing better suited to destroy the foundations of society than to make an unflagging attack upon the Church of God, to bring her into discredit and odium by spreading infamous calumnies, and accusing her of being opposed to genuine progress. They labor to weaken her influence and power by wounds daily inflicted, and to overthrow the authority of the Bishop of Rome, in whom the abiding and unchangeable principles of right and good find their earthly guardian and champion.[4]

In Catholic belief, the pope has been granted a special gift to discern and teach the natural moral law "infallibly." This does not mean that no one else can discern the truths of the natural moral law. It is, paradoxically, an infallible teaching of the Catholic Church that the natural moral law can be known in its fullness by all human beings through the use of reason unaided by faith.[5] The "fullness of truth" that the Catholic Church claims refers to matters of faith, not of morals exclusively — as is logical, if we think about it. After all, why would any organized religion claim to teach a revelation from God that it did not also claim was completely or fully true?

No, Leo XIII was clearly referring not to matters of faith, but of morals, the natural moral law, and the undermining of the natural law in part by attacking the institution that believes itself to be the chief teacher and defender of the natural moral law. Nor do we have to be Catholic or even Christian to appreciate the seriousness of the attack on the teaching authority of the Catholic Church. Matters of faith are, as far as the civil order is concerned, a matter of opinion. As de Tocqueville pointed

---

[4] *Inscrutabili*, § 3.
[5] Pius XII, *Humani Generis* ("Concerning Some False Opinions Threatening to Undermine the Foundations of Catholic Doctrine"), 1950, § 2.

out, as long as the purely religious teachings — matters of
faith — of a sect or religion do no harm to the common
good and are consistent with the natural moral law, and
the State does not itself transgress the precepts of the
natural law, then the State has as much business interfering in the internal affairs of that religion as that religion has interfering in civil matters — that is, none at all.

The Natural Law

The case is different with the precepts of the natural
moral law. While taught in large measure by organized
religion, the natural moral law is, as we have seen, the
basis of a just social order. Prior to the shift away from
the Aristotelian/Thomist understanding of the natural
law that occurred in the 16th century, the precepts of the
law were universally accepted in the west, and (in different forms) in the east as well, as C. S. Lewis demonstrated in *The Abolition of Man* (1943). Applications of the precepts of the natural law may vary, even widely at times,
as people adapt the broad outline of the law to meet their
particular needs, wants, social conditions, and so on. The
basic precepts, however, remain unchanged. As Heinrich
Rommen explained, using the institution of private property as an example,

> Only the legal institutions of private property and in-
> heritance are of natural law. That is to say, the natu-
> ral law requires only that there be private ownership
> and the right of inheritance. It does not demand the
> property and inheritance institutions of feudalism, or
> of liberalist capitalism, or of a system in which pri-
> vate, corporate, and public forms of ownership exist
> side by side. These are positive-law determinations
> which spring from the diversity of peoples and which
> change with the socioeconomic evolution.[6]

To counter the anti-human effects of undermining the
moral authority of the Catholic Church, Leo XIII advocat-

---

[6] *The Natural Law*, 209.

ed restoring the teaching of the natural law in the schools, especially to young children:

> The more the enemies of religion exert themselves to offer the uninformed, especially the young, such instruction as darkens the mind and corrupts morals, the more actively should we endeavor that not only a suitable and solid method of education may flourish, but above all that this education be wholly in harmony with the Catholic faith in its literature and system of training, and chiefly in philosophy, upon which the foundation of other sciences in great measure depends. Philosophy seeks not the overthrow of divine revelation, but delights rather to prepare its way, and defend it against assailants, both by example and in written works.[7]

Having identified the underlying cause of the evils of modern society, in *Quod Apostolici Muneris* (1878), his second encyclical, Leo XIII singled out specific evils — "Socialism, Communism, Nihilism" — for special attention. Nor should it come as a surprise, once we understand the reasons for this concern. As Leo XIII stated,

> The natural union of man and woman, which is held sacred even among barbarous nations, they hold in scorn; and its bond, whereby family life is chiefly maintained, they slacken, or else yield up to the sway of lust. In short, spurred on by greedy hankering after things present, which is *the root of all evils, which some coveting have erred from the faith*,[8] they attack the right of property, sanctioned by the law of nature, and with signal depravity, while pretending to feel solicitous about the needs, and anxious to satisfy the requirements of all, they strain every effort to seize upon and hold in common all that has been individually

---

[7] *Inscrutabili* § 13.
[8] 1 Tim. vi 10.

acquired by title of lawful inheritance, through intellectual or manual labor, or economy in living.[9]

The balance of the encyclical is concerned with demolishing all the excuses used by socialists, communists, and nihilists to abolish private property, either by redefining it, or by outright confiscation. There is an astonishingly brief exhortation to the rich to alleviate the distress of the poor by distributing alms out of their superabundance,[10] but also a reminder that it is God's part, not man's, to punish greed and the refusal to distribute superfluous wealth.

Leo XIII's third encyclical, *Æterni Patris* ("On the Study of Scholastic Philosophy"), 1879, was a strong reminder (just in case anyone still had any doubts) that the natural moral law as defined by Aquinas — that is, the natural moral law based on the Intellect (Nature), not the Will — is the only sound basis for a just social order.

The problem was that people still didn't appear to be "getting it." Clearly something had to be done. That "something" is what we will look at in the next chapter.

---

[9] *Quod Apostolici Muneris* § 3.
[10] *Ibid.*, § 11.

13. Leo XIII and America

Despite a series of encyclicals clearly intended to reorient the social order back into conformity with the natural moral law, very few people seemed to understand what it was that Pope Leo XIII was trying to do. Such encyclicals as *Arcanum Divinae* ("On Christian Marriage"), *Humanum Genus* ("On Freemasonry"), *Libertas Praestantissimum* ("On Human Liberty"), *Exeunte Jam Anno* ("On the Right Ordering of Christian Life"), and *Sapientiae Christianae* ("On the Chief Duties of Christians as Citizens") all addressed various political issues from within the framework of the natural moral law as found in the philosophy of Aristotle and Aquinas.

Human Dignity

The purpose of these encyclicals was to restore respect for the dignity of each human person, manifested by rebuilding and restoring the institutions of the social order in a manner consistent with the sovereignty of the individual under God. Unfortunately, most people read their own opinions into the encyclicals. As a result, they constructed private interpretations based in large measure on individual faith and private systems of morals. Consciously or unconsciously, they edited out anything that contradicted their deeply held beliefs, especially in the area of politics and economics. As Emmanuel Mounier noted with unconscious irony in *A Personalist Manifesto,*

> The moralizers are no less dangerous. Like the doctrinaires they are strangers to the living reality that is history [that is, the institutions of the social order, inextricably rooted in the past as well as existing in the present], and they oppose it, not by a rational system, but by moral demands of the widest generality. They do not try to influence living history by means of a strong spiritual structure which could give rise to a

program of definite action through a profound knowledge of the needs and the techniques of the present day [a reference to "Catholic Action" as restructured by Pope Pius XI]. Instead they are content above all to spend their energies in a vigorous eloquence that is as full of good will as it is ineffective. Some of them try to go beyond moral preaching. They launch upon a sharp spiritual critique of the evil forces or tendencies. But when they enter upon a constructive technique, they seem to think of nothing but moral weapons and above all only of individual moral efforts. They harmonize the purest suppositions in a most naïve manner. They properly exhort individuals to cultivate the virtues which give strength to social life. But they forget that historical forces [institutions], freed from submission to the spiritual [the natural moral law], have created collective structures and material necessities [*i.e.*, institutions and our social duties] that we must inevitably reckon with insofar as "the spiritual itself is embodied in flesh." Such men are a constant source of danger, since they tend to lead the spiritual forces, which we should like to inject into history [*i.e.*, into our institutions], above or around the historical happenings without coming to grips with them.[1]

Keeping in mind these common assumptions, it should come as no surprise that with the issue of *Rerum Novarum* ("On Labor and Capital") in 1891, many people assumed that the pope was doing something new and different. Blind to the fact that there are no teachings in *Rerum Novarum* that did not already appear in other encyclicals, most people seem to have missed the obvious point that the only difference between *Rerum Novarum* and previous documents is that *Rerum Novarum* gives an explicit remedy for the perceived conflicts in society: widespread di-

---

[1] Emmanuel Mounier, *A Personalist Manifesto*. London: Longmans, Green and Co., 1938, 4-5.

rect ownership of the means of production. As the pope clearly explained,

> We have seen that this great labor question cannot be solved save by assuming as a principle that private ownership must be held sacred and inviolable. The law, therefore, should favor ownership, and its policy should be to induce as many as possible of the people to become owners.[2]

Property Yet Again

The first sentence in this quote contains no surprises. It simply restates what was said in previous encyclicals and stressed almost to the point of redundancy in *Rerum Novarum* itself. The cause of so many problems in the world is the rejection or redefinition of the natural moral law, particularly with respect to the institution of private property, one of the primary natural rights.

The second sentence, however, contains the "radical" part of *Rerum Novarum*. Previous teachings had simply exhorted the rich to distribute a measure of their surplus wealth to alleviate poverty. Now, however, here was an explicit command — not a "prudential suggestion" as some panic-stricken commentators, socialist in all but name, characterized it! — that it is not enough to distribute alms. The rich, the whole of society acting through its chief agent for the care of the common good, the State, is to reorganize itself so as to promote not simply the alleviation of poverty, but its eradication. How? By somehow opening up democratic access to the means of acquiring and possessing private property in the means of production so that ordinary people can participate to the fullest extent possible in the economic common good.

In the same paragraph, however, Leo XIII made a fatal error — or (at least) other people have fatally misunderstood just how far the pope's teaching authority and infallibility extends, and where an infallible teaching leaves off and prudential matter begins. The paragraph begins,

---

[2] § 46.

"If a workman's wages be sufficient to enable him comfortably to support himself, his wife, and his children, he will find it easy, if he be a sensible man, to practice thrift, and he will not fail, by cutting down expenses, to put by some little savings and thus secure a modest source of income."

That is, the pope appears to be telling us how capital formation is financed: cut consumption, save, then invest. This is, indeed, the manner in which the British Currency School claimed is the only way that capital formation can be financed, and is embodied as a virtual religious doctrine in Keynesian economics. It assumes as a given that "money" is correctly defined as a purchase order issued or authorized by the State. This understanding of money, as we have already seen, when taken to its logical conclusion effectively abolishes private property and is thus inconsistent with the natural moral law.

Even if you happen to be a fanatical Catholic, it is evident that the pope can be wrong when speaking outside his area of competence. The pope is not an expert in economics and finance, nor is it disrespectful to point this out. The specific means by which workers or anyone else become owners is irrelevant as long as the means is moral as well as practicable. That is all we need to know.

Universal Truths

We should be prepared, then, as rational human beings, to discern the universal truths in these teachings as well as those of any other moral authorities of all faiths, and apply them as justice and prudence dictate. Consistent with the theory that society is at its most healthy (economically and politically just) when individuals and the institutions of the whole of the common good comply as far as possible with the precepts of the natural moral law, there are certain goals necessarily to be sought through acts of social justice. We can call these the "Four Pillars of an Economically Just Society." These are:

A limited economic role for the State. If, consistent with Catholic and other moral teaching, we reject State absolutism and accept democratic principles, both common sense and the principle of subsidiarity dictate that much of what people have allowed the State to usurp, especially in matters of personal economy (what the Germans call "Volkswirtshaft"[3]), is now the responsibility of individuals, either alone or (more usually) in free association with others. The State's proper role is limited to ensuring that everyone has an equal opportunity and the means to meet his or her material needs and those of his or her dependents adequately and securely. The State carries out its proper function by lifting barriers that inhibit or prevent full participation in the common good. As a general rule, the State should never do anything that the citizens, individually or in free association, can do for themselves. To guard against the abuse of the State's legitimate monopoly over the instruments of coercion, the State must at all times be economically dependent on its citizens, not the other way around. As an expedient in an emergency, the State may undertake to guarantee individual welfare, thereby imposing a temporary condition of dependency, but this must be regarded only as a last resort, and must cease as soon as private means of succor become available, especially through an individual's own efforts.

Free and open markets as the best means of determining just wages, just prices, and just profits. In his social doctrine, Pius XI emphasized seemingly to the point of redundancy the principle of "free association," that is, liberty. If we are as individual human beings charged with the responsibility for the common good, and we can only affect the common good through acts of social justice carried out by organizing with others, then it necessarily follows that not the State, other individuals or groups, nor society as a whole can interfere with the right of free association, except as required to prevent material harm to

---

[3] Sometimes misleadingly translated as "National Economy."

individuals, groups, or the common good as a whole. Free and open markets, as the means of ensuring that personal choice, as an exercise of personal sovereignty and expression of human dignity, ultimately dominates within a sound moral and strong juridical order, are essential to making the institutions of money and credit operate for the good of all rather than exclusively for the State or the State's favored individuals or groups. We necessarily understand "money" in this context as whatever anyone will accept in settlement of a debt, and do not limit the definition to State-issued or authorized purchase orders. Further, the dignity of the human person demands that, as soon as someone gains the status of non-dependent adult, he or she must have an equal opportunity to participate freely to the fullest extent possible in the common good, of which economics constitutes an important part.

Recognition and protection of the rights of private property. With the rapid economic disenfranchisement of the great mass of people through being stripped of both private property in the means of production, and the means of acquiring that property in the first place, it would be more accurate to rephrase this necessary goal as "restoration of the rights of private property," and (in recognition of the fact that the business corporation is the predominant form of economic organization) add "particularly in corporate equity." From the early 20th century, due largely to misleading definitions of money and credit and methods of corporate finance employed, minority shareholders had been stripped of their natural right of control and the enjoyment of the fruits of ownership. Thus, even when people owned a moderate stake of income-generating assets, the ownership was in many cases so attenuated as to be effectively meaningless. "Property," however, is not the thing owned, but the right to be an owner, as well as the bundle of rights that define how an owner may use what he or she possesses

— particularly with respect to how what is owned can be used, and receipt of the income (*i.e.*, "profit") the asset generates.

Widespread direct ownership of the means of production. If the general necessity of restoring the natural moral law based on the Intellect (Nature) as the basis of a just social order and the foundation of respect for the dignity of the human person can be said to have a "rival" on the list of papal goals, it is the particular necessity of ensuring that "the law, therefore, should favor ownership, and its policy should be to induce as many as possible of the people to become owners."[4] The sheer number of papal statements regarding the importance, even necessity of widespread direct ownership of the means of production render it incredible that anyone could possibly reinterpret the clear teachings of the popes as advocating some form of socialism, that is, the abolition of private property. That, however, is the case in an overwhelming number of instances. Despite the hysteria with which papal teachings on private property are opposed, reinterpreted, ignored, and so on, however, there is no more effective means of empowering the human person to carry out acts of social justice and therefore assume his or her responsibility for the care of the common good at his or her level, than ownership of the means of production. Ownership also serves to protect and maintain all other rights, especially life and liberty. As William Cobbett declared, "Freedom is not an empty sound; it is not an abstract idea; it is not a thing that nobody can feel. It means, — and it means nothing else, — the full and quiet enjoyment of your own property. If you have not this, if this be not well secured to you, you may call yourself what you will, but you are a slave.[5]

---

[4] *Rerum Novarum*, § 46.
[5] *A History of the Protestant Reformation in England and Ireland*, 1826, §456.

Social Justice

Putting these Four Pillars of an Economically Just Society together, we see their conformity to the three principles of economic justice developed by Louis Kelso and Mortimer Adler as well as with social justice as developed by Pius XI and analyzed by Ferree. The three principles of economic justice are 1) Distribution (Distributive Justice), 2) Participation (Participatory Justice) and 3) Harmony (Social Justice). Kelso and Adler used the term "Limitation." We prefer the term "Harmony" as more descriptive of the application of the principle.

We now have (at least in outline) all that we need to realize our human nature both as individuals and as members of society. The act of social justice is the social tool by means of which we can realize our political nature and act together in solidarity for the mutual advantage of ourselves as individuals, and everyone else as members of society. As Orestes Brownson put it, we must strive to attain "the sovereignty of the people without social despotism, and individual freedom without anarchy."

In the next and final chapter, we will take a look at Capital Homesteading, a proposal that appears to have the potential to effect the restructuring of the economic order — and thus the political order — so as to start the process of bringing the whole of the common good back into material conformity with the precepts of the natural moral law.

14. Capital Homesteading

In the previous chapter, we asserted that Capital Homesteading has the potential to initiate the restructuring of the social order in the economic realm as the solution to Keynesian monetary and fiscal errors. Capital Homesteading addresses the two primary areas on which moral authorities have focused attention: the restoration of the natural law as the basis of a just society, and the natural right to private property as an essential prop for the other natural rights, especially life, liberty (free association), and the pursuit of happiness (the acquisition and development of virtue).

Restructuring of the Social Order

Often thought in the modern world to be completely unrelated, even antithetical to the restoration of a just society, the restoration of morality and widespread direct ownership of the means of production go hand-in-hand, as moral authorities through the ages have recognized. The problems facing modern society cannot be solved and the natural moral law restored except through the action of ordinary people organizing for the common good. Further, ordinary people will never have the power to organize effectively until and unless they have direct ownership of a meaningful stake of income-generating assets. As Daniel Webster observed in 1820, "Power naturally and necessarily follows property."[1]

The problem is how to empower ordinary people with the means of acquiring and possessing private property and thereby lay the groundwork for solving today's problems. In a modern economy, that necessarily means democratic access to money and credit by reforming the money and credit system.

---

[1] Massachusetts Constitutional Convention.

Unfortunately, the modern understanding of money and credit results in the erroneous belief that only existing accumulations of savings can be used to finance capital formation. By right of private property, this necessarily restricts ownership of all newly formed capital to those who, by definition, have a monopoly on existing accumulations of savings: the rich.

Capital Homesteading is specifically designed to solve this problem. First, of course, Capital Homesteading uses a different understanding of money and credit than found in prevailing theories. This is a more organic, natural understanding based on the laws of social justice, especially freedom of association.

We necessarily have to discard the idea embodied in Keynesian economics that "money" is exclusively a State creation. This is an inorganic and legalistic concept that permits the State to finance its activities without having to obtain the consent of the taxpayer. It turns money into a purchase order issued by the State or a State-authorized individual or institution. When the economy needs more "money," the State creates more; when there is too much, the State reduces the amount through taxation.

Consequently, we must restore Say's Law of Markets and its application in the "real bills doctrine" as part of an overall reform of the financial system. The real bills doctrine is that money can be created as necessary to carry out transactions without inflation or deflation, as long as the new money is backed by the present value of existing inventories or a future stream of income to be realized from the production of marketable goods and services.)

Understanding Money

Capital Homesteading accepts Say's Law and the real bills doctrine. This is a different, more natural understanding of money than is found in Keynesian economics or any of the other major schools of economics. The understanding of money in Capital Homesteading is more consistent with the tenets of the British Banking School. As we have seen, this is that "money" is whatever is or can be accepted by anyone in settlement of a debt. Money is therefore necessarily linked through the institution of private property to the present value of existing and future marketable goods and services in the economy.

Keynes's unproved assertions in Volume I of his *Treatise on Money* to the contrary, the parties to the transaction who have a direct private property interest in the value or claims being conveyed by the money, not the State, make the determination as to what constitutes money. The State may make a declaration that something will be exclusively accepted by the State in payment of taxes, or that such and such a thing, if delivered under certain conditions, satisfies a debt if there is some dispute in the matter. The State cannot, however, under any circumstances declare a contract or other transaction void simply because it does not involve State-issued or authorized currency, or is undertaken without the explicit consent of the State.

The State's role is to regulate the value of the currency, create a uniform standard of measure, and to police abuses that may occur in the process of money creation. This, obviously, is not a creative function of the State. Asserting that the State, because it has the responsibility for setting and maintaining a uniform standard and to police abuses, legitimately has the power to create money or arbitrarily set the amount of money, is not logical. It is the same as if the State, charged with setting the standards for a uniform system of weights and measures, declared that only a limited number of inches could be used in the coming year. If anything else needs to be measured, application must be made to the State for a new issue of rulers and yardsticks. Louis Kelso perhaps said it best when he pointed out,

> Money is not a part of the visible sector of the economy; people do not consume money. Money is not a physical factor of production, but rather a yardstick for measuring economic input, economic outtake and the relative values of the real goods and services of the economic world. Money provides a method of

measuring obligations, rights, powers and privileges. It provides a means whereby certain individuals can accumulate claims against others, or against the economy as a whole, or against many economies. It is a system of symbols that many economists substitute for the visible sector and its productive enterprises, goods and services, thereby losing sight of the fact that a monetary system is a part only of the invisible sector of the economy, and that its adequacy can *only* be measured by its effect upon the visible sector.[2]

Obviously, then, believing that the State has the power actually to create money on its own authority without producing anything ("economic input") is to put the State in the position of having absolute power. The only problem this solves is how the current financial and political elite is to maintain itself in power. This is just as Keynes intimated in his *Treatise on Money* with his declaration that the State has the right to "re-edit the dictionary," *i.e.*, alter reality to suit itself. It is the logical outcome of the Knapp's chartalism, in which only unbacked State-issued tokens and notes are considered money, and no one may transact business of any kind without the explicit consent of the State.[3]

Such power has only one result: the creation of an elite that, while not themselves owners of the money issued by the State in the name of "the people" (*never* actual people), puts control over money and credit in their hands, "which they administer according to their own arbitrary will and pleasure."[4]

The chief problem, then, is not the inability to produce, nor is manipulating the currency and the tax system the solution. As Dr. Harold Moulton pointed out in *America's*

[2] Louis O. Kelso, *Two-Factor Theory: The Economics of Reality*. New York: Random House, 1967, 54.
[3] Knapp, *op. cit.*
[4] *Quadragesimo Anno, op. cit.*, § 105.

Capacity to Produce,[5] America — the world — has demonstrated time and again that the economy typically operates at much less than full productive capacity. Nor is it a problem of lack of consumer demand, as Moulton explained in *America's Capacity to Consume*.[6] Every individual living at or below the poverty level argues otherwise.

Politicizing Money and Credit

No, the problem is that the money and credit system, which is designed and intended to link together production and consumption, has been diverted to other purposes. This is usually done to further political aims or implement some variety of social engineering to transform society into the vision (or lack thereof) of the latest administration in Washington. Money and credit have been redefined to serve the needs of either a private elite, as in capitalism, or a State elite, as in socialism.

Capitalism establishes a monopoly over money and credit — and thus access to the means of acquiring and possessing private property in the means of production — by insisting that only existing accumulations of savings can be used to finance capital formation. Socialism establishes a monopoly over money and credit by insisting that only the State has the right to create money.

Moulton demonstrated the falsity of the capitalist claim in 1935 in *The Formation of Capital*. More than a century earlier Jean-Baptiste Say refuted the socialist position when he proved that "money," just as Kelso pointed out in *Two-Factor Theory*,[7] is not a State monopoly. Instead, money is a symbol for what we and others produce, invented to facilitate the exchange of those productions among people, just as Aristotle claimed in *The Politics*.

---

[5] Harold G. Moulton, *America's Capacity to Produce*. Washington, DC: The Brookings Institution, 1934.
[6] Harold G. Moulton, *America's Capacity to Consume*. Washington, DC: The Brookings Institution, 1934.
[7] *Op. cit.*

In view of the wasted productive capacity evident in all economies and the manifest under-consumption revealed by the existence of poverty (to which we add our understanding of money and credit as an organized and regulated means of linking production and consumption through the institution of private property), the solution becomes obvious. The money and credit system must be reformed to open up democratic access to the means of acquiring and possessing private property in the means of production. That is what Capital Homesteading proposes to do.

Good Credit v. Bad Credit

Today even the poor have little or no trouble buying consumer goods and services on credit. So distorted has economic policy become that consumer credit — which many people have no real hope of repaying — has become the driving force of the economy. Making matters worse, these purchases are not income-generating assets. As a general rule, while capital credit can make someone wealthy, consumer credit makes the borrower even more economically vulnerable than before.

Consider the fact that even in a "slow growth" economy, America adds annually approximately $2 trillion worth of new productive assets in both the public sector and private sector. This works out to around $7,000 for every man, woman, and child. Under both capitalist and socialist assumptions these assets are typically financed in ways that create few if any new owners. The gap between "haves" and "have-nots" continues to widen.

There is an alternative to capitalism and socialism and a solution to this failure of the financial system to serve the needs of common, ordinary people. This "Just Third Way" is a natural law-based, free enterprise economy, generating private sector profits. The Just Third Way "difference," and the heart of the solution, is that the ownership of the new growth would flow directly to every individual citizen.

With democratic access to capital credit repayable with the full pre-tax earnings of the capital itself, everyone could gain ownership in America's expanding technological frontier. We would not have to take away wealth from those who already own capital to provide ownership, nor have the State redistribute income to make up for the lack of widespread direct capital ownership. The principal vehicle for achieving these goals is the proposed "Capital Homestead Act."

The Means of Acquiring and Possessing Property

The Capital Homestead Act is a modern analogue of Lincoln's 1862 Homestead Act. The original Act offered a piece of the land frontier to anyone 21 years of age or older, and who was an American citizen or stated the intention to become a citizen. The Homestead Act was the most successful economic initiative in America's history. It laid the foundation for America's rise as the world's greatest industrial power.

Unfortunately, the land frontier ran out. Nor were most Americans ever given a chance to share in the ownership and profits of our high-tech industrial frontier, which, unlike land, has no known limits.

Capital Homesteading would take nothing away from present owners. Instead, Capital Homesteading would link every American (including the poorest of the poor) from the moment of birth to the profits from sustainable economic growth. Every worker and citizen could gain a share in power over technological progress and the tools and enterprises of modern society. Through widespread ownership all citizens would participate in a more democratic economic process, just as they now participate in the democratic political process through access to the ballot.

The proposed Capital Homestead Act embodies a number of programs that would enable every man, woman, and child to obtain interest- (but not cost-) free capital credit from a local bank or other financial institution. Future earnings of the capital would pay off the loans, including bank service fees and premiums to cover capital credit default insurance. Through the Capital Homestead Act, access to capital credit — which today helps make the rich richer — would be enshrined in law as a fundamental right of citizenship, like the right to vote.

Reform of the Central Bank

Using its powers under § 13 of the Federal Reserve Act, the Federal Reserve System would supply local banks with the money needed by businesses to grow — but only in exchange for financially feasible investments brought to the banks for financing. This is a critical reform of the money and credit system that is often overlooked: money could not be created until and unless it is backed 100% by the present value of existing assets or the future stream of income to be generated by an investment, and accepted as such in commerce.

Trapped by the dogmatic belief that capital formation can only be financed using existing accumulations of savings, today's economists and banking experts assume as a matter of course that money must first be created before investment can take place. Inflation then shifts the purchasing power of existing savings to the investor, who uses it to finance the new capital.

The monetary reforms of Capital Homesteading counter such institutionalized and systemic plutocracy by requiring that any new money must be backed by the present value of existing or future marketable goods and services. No money can be created — a contract accepted — until and unless there is a reasonable assurance that the assets financed will, in fact, generate a stream of profits sufficient to repay and cancel the money created to finance the capital formation in the first place, and thereafter provide consumption income for the owner of the asset. This is nothing more than the real bills doctrine embodied in the tenets of the British Banking School.

The difference between Capital Homesteading and classic banking theory is that the new money and credit for private sector growth would be "irrigated" through Capital Homestead Accounts and other credit democratization vehicles. Using conservative projections, this could result in a child born today under Capital Homesteading accumulating nearly $500,000 in income-generating assets by age 65, and enjoying approximately $1.6 million in dividend income over the same period.

Through a well-regulated central banking system and other safeguards (including capital credit insurance to cover the risk of bad loans), all citizens could purchase with interest-free capital credit, newly issued shares representing newly added machines and structures. These purchases would be paid off with tax-deductible dividends of these companies. Neither existing accumulations of savings nor current consumption income would be reduced.

Thus, Capital Homesteading is an application of the principles of the natural moral law as they pertain to money, credit, and finance, and a blueprint for restructuring the social order. Capital Homesteading provides a means to get away from false and dehumanizing definitions of money and credit, putting these uniquely social goods at the service of the whole of humanity instead of a small elite.

Bibliography

Church Documents

Gregory XVI, *In Supremo* ("On the Slave Trade"), 1839.

Leo XIII, *Quod Apostolici Muneris* ("On Socialism, Communism, Nihilism"), 1878.

Leo XIII, *Inscrutabili* ("On the Evils Afflicting Modern Society"), 1878.

Leo XIII, *Æterni Patris* ("On the Study of Scholastic Philosophy"), 1879.

Leo XIII, *Arcanum Divinae* ("On Christian Marriage"), 1880.

Leo XIII, *Humanum Genus* ("On Freemasonry"), 1884.

Leo XIII, *Exeunte Jam Anno* ("On the Right Ordering of Christian Life"), 1888.

Leo XIII, *Libertas Praestantissimum* ("On Human Liberty"), 1888.

Leo XIII, *Sapientiae Christianae* ("On the Chief Duties of Christians as Citizens"), 1890.

Leo XIII, *Rerum Novarum* ("On Labor and Capital"), 1891.

Leo XIII, *Testem Benevolentia* ("Concerning New Opinions, Virtue, Nature and Grace, with Regard to Americanism"), 1899.

Pius XI, *Ubi Arcano Dei Consilio* ("On the Peace of Christ in the Kingdom of Christ"), 1922.

Pius XI, *Quas Primas* ("On the Feast of Christ the King"), 1925.

Pius XI, *Quadragesimo Anno* ("On the Restructuring of the Social Order"), 1931.

Pius XI, *Divini Redemptoris* ("On Atheistic Communism"), 1937.

Pius XII, *Humani Generis* ("Concerning Some False Opinions Threatening to Undermine the Foundations of Catholic Doctrine"), 1950

Books

Aquinas, St. Thomas, *De Regimine Principum*. Toronto, Canada: St. Michael's College, 1935.

Aquinas, St. Thomas, *The Summa Theologica*. Westminster, Maryland: Christian Classics, 1948.

Aristotle, *The Athenian Constitution*. London: Penguin Books, 1984.

Aristotle, *The Nichomachean Ethics*. Buffalo, New York: Prometheus Books, 1987.

Aristotle, *The Politics*. London: Penguin Books, 1981.

Attwater, Donald, *The Avenel Dictionary of Saints*. New York: Avenel Books, 1981.

Bagehot, Walter, *Lombard Street: A Description of the Money Market*. New York: Scribner, Armstrong, and Co., 1874.

Bagehot, Walter, *The English Constitution*. Brighton, UK: Sussex Academic Press, 1997.

Bellarmine, St. Robert, *De Laicis, or, The Treatise on Civil Government*. Westport, Connecticut: Hyperion Press, Inc., 1928.

Belloc, Hilaire, *How the Reformation Happened*. Magnolia, Massachusetts: Peter Smith Publishers, Inc., 1975.

Brodrick, James, S.J., *Robert Bellarmine: Saint and Scholar*. Westminster, UK: The Newman Press, 1961.

Brownson, Orestes, *Essays and Reviews Chiefly on Theology, Politics, and Socialism*, 1852.

Brownson, Orestes, *The American Republic*. New York: P. O'Shea, 1865.

Cahill, Rev. Eamon, *The Framework of a Christian State*. Dublin, Éire: M. H. Gill and Son, Ltd., 1932.

Chesterton, G. K., *Saint Thomas Aquinas: "The Dumb Ox."* New York: Image Books, 1956.

Christy, David, *Cotton is King*. New York: Derby and Jackson, 1856.

Civardi, Luigi, *Manual of Catholic Action*. New York: Sheed and Ward, 1936.

Cobbett, William, *A History of the Protestant Reformation in England and Ireland*, 1826.

Conant, Charles A., *A History of Modern Banks of Issue*. New York: G. P. Putnam's Sons, 1927.

Crook, J. A., *Law and Life of Rome, 90 B.C. — A.D. 212*. Ithaca, New York: Cornell University Press, 1967.

Dicey, Albert Venn, *A Digest of the Law of England with Reference to the Conflict of Laws*. London: Stevens, 1958.

Dicey, Albert Venn, *Introduction to the Study of the Law of the Constitution*. Indianapolis, Indiana: Liberty Fund, Inc., 1982.

Dicey, Albert Venn, *Lectures on the Relation Between Law and Public Opinion in England During the Nineteenth Century*. New Brunswick, New Jersey: Transaction Books, 1981.

Einhard and Notker the Stammerer, *Two Lives of Charlemagne*. London: Penguin Books, 1969.

Ferree, Rev. William J., S.M., Ph.D., *Introduction to Social Justice*. Arlington, Virginia: Economic Justice Media, 1998.

Ferree, Rev. William J., S.M., Ph.D., *The Act of Social Justice*. Washington, DC: Catholic University of America Press, 1943.

Figgis, John Neville, *The Divine Right of Kings*. Bristol, UK: Thoemmes Press, 1994.

Filmer, Sir Robert, *Patriarcha and Other Writings*. Cambridge, UK: Cambridge University Press, 1991.

Fisher, Irving, *The Purchasing Power of Money*. New York: Macmillan, 1931.

Greaney, Michael D., *In Defense of Human Dignity*. Arlington, Virginia: Economic Justice Media, 2008.

Henri, Florette, *George Mason of Virginia*. New York: Crowell-Collier Press, 1971.

Hill, Helen, *George Mason, Constitutionalist*. Cambridge, Massachusetts: Harvard University Press, 1938.

Hobbes, Thomas, *Leviathan, or, The Matter, Form, and Power of a Commonwealth Ecclesiastical and Civil*. London: Penguin Books, 1985.

Kaplan, Edward S., *The Bank of the United States and the American Economy*. Westport, Connecticut: Greenwood Press, 1999.

Kelly, J. N. D., *The Oxford Dictionary of Popes*. Oxford, UK: Oxford University Press, 1986.

Kelso, Louis, and Adler, Mortimer, *The Capitalist Manifesto*. New York: Random House, 1958.

Kelso, Louis, and Adler, Mortimer, *The New Capitalists: A Proposal to Free Economic Growth from the Slavery of Savings.* New York: Random House, 1961.

Kelso, Louis, *Two-Factor Theory: The Economics of Reality.* New York: Random House, 1967.

Keynes, John Maynard, *A Treatise on Money, Volume I: The Pure Theory of Money.* New York: Harcourt, Brace and Company, 1930.

Keynes, John Maynard, *The Economic Consequences of the Peace.* London: Penguin Books, 1988.

Knapp, Georg Friedrich, *The State Theory of Money.* London: Macmillan & Company, Ltd., 1924.

Kouns, Nathan C., *Arius the Libyan, An Idyl of the Primitive Church.* New York: D. Appleton and Company, 1922.

Kouns, Nathan C., *Dorcas, the Daughter of Faustina.* San Francisco, California: John Howell, 1922.

Kurland, Norman G., Brohawn, Dawn K., Greaney, Michael D., *Capital Homesteading for Every Citizen.* Arlington, Virginia: Economic Justice Media, 2004.

Locke, John, *First and Second Treatises on Government.* Cambridge, UK: Cambridge University Press, 1960.

Marx, Karl, *The Communist Manifesto.* London: Penguin Books, 1967.

Miller, Rev. John H., C.S.C., S.T.D., *Curing World Poverty.* St. Louis, Missouri: Social Justice Review, 1994.

Morrison, Charles, *An Essay on the Relations Between Labour and Capital.* London: Longman, Brown, Green, and Longmans, 1854.

Moulton, Harold, *America's Capacity to Consume.* Washington, DC: The Brookings Institution, 1934.

Moulton, Harold, *America's Capacity to Produce.* Washington, DC: The Brookings Institution, 1934.

Moulton, Harold, *Income and Economic Progress.* Washington, DC: The Brookings Institution, 1935.

Moulton, Harold, *The Formation of Capital.* Washington, DC: The Brookings Institution, 1935.

Moulton, Harold, *Financial Organization and the Economic System*. New York: McGraw-Hill Book Company, 1938.

Mounier, Emmanuel, *A Personalist Manifesto*. London: Longmans, Green and Co., 1938.

Panzer, Rev. Joel S., *The Popes and Slavery*. New York: Alba House, 1996.

Rager, Rev. John Clement, *The Political Philosophy of Blessed Robert Bellarmine*. Spokane, Washington: The Apostolate of Our Lady of Siluva, 1995.

Rommen, Heinrich, *The Natural Law*. Indianapolis, Indiana: Liberty Fund, Inc., 1998.

Rommen, Heinrich, *The State in Catholic Thought*. St. Louis, Missouri: B. Herder Book Co., 1947.

Rutland, Robert A., *George Mason: Reluctant Statesman*. Baton Rouge, Louisiana: Louisiana State University Press, 1961.

Say, Jean-Baptiste, *Letters to Mr. Malthus on Several Subjects of Political Economy and on the Cause of the Stagnation of Commerce*. London: Sherwood, Neely & Jones, 1821.

Sidney, Algernon, *Discourses Concerning Government*. Indianapolis, Indiana: Liberty Fund, Inc., 1990.

Smith, Adam, *The Theory of Moral Sentiments*. Indianapolis, Indiana: Liberty Fund, Inc., 1976.

Smith, Adam, *The Wealth of Nations*. Indianapolis, Indiana: Liberty Fund, Inc., 1981.

Tocqueville, Alexis de, *Democracy in America*. New York: Alfred A. Knopf, 1994.

Torre, Teodoro de la, *Popular History of Philosophy*. Houston, Texas: Lumen Christi Press, 1988.

Wooten, David, ed., *Divine Right and Democracy: An Anthology of Political Writing in Stuart England*. London: Penguin Books, 1986.

Index

CPSIA information can be obtained
at www.ICGtesting.com
Printed in the USA
FFOW04n1910240914
7519FF